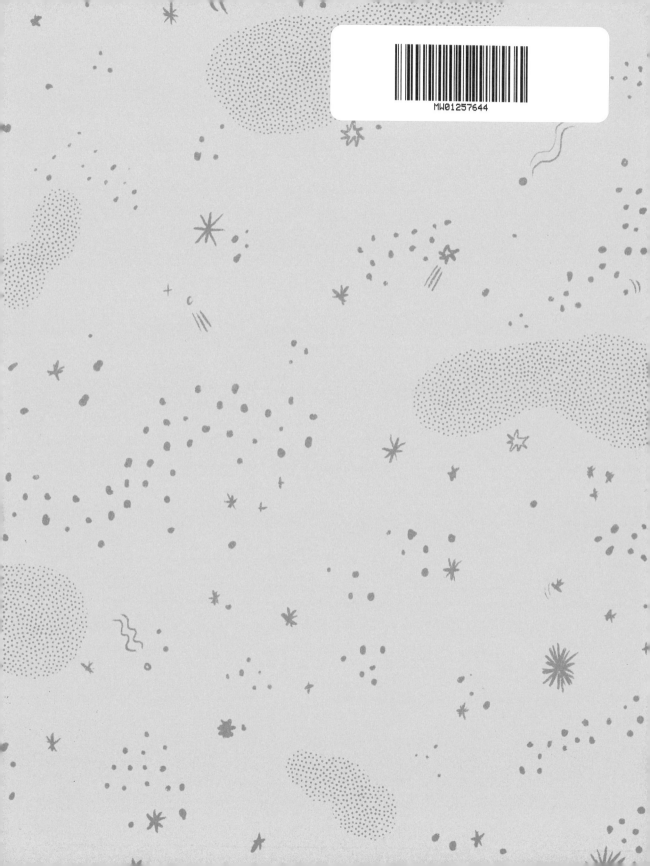

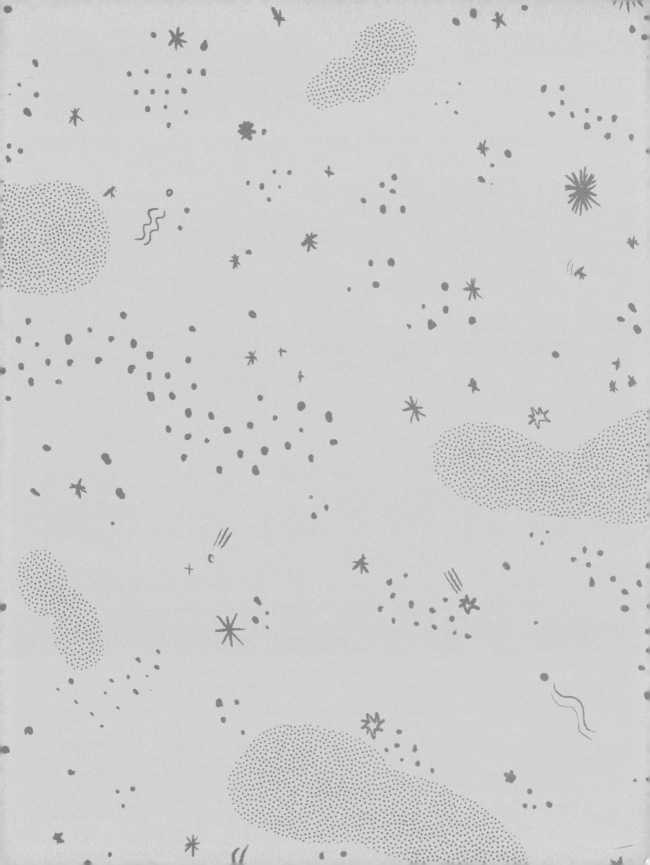

the
BOOK
of
BELONGING

BELOVED

BELONGING

DELIGHTFUL

the
BOOK
of
BELONGING

BIBLE STORIES *for*
KIND & CONTEMPLATIVE KIDS

WORDS *by*
MARIKO CLARK

PICTURES *by*
RACHEL ELEANOR

CONVERGENT

Published in the United States by Convergent Books, an imprint of Random House,
a division of Penguin Random House LLC, New York.

CONVERGENT BOOKS is a registered trademark, and the Convergent colophon
is a trademark of Penguin Random House LLC.

Library of Congress Cataloging-in-Publication Data
Names: Clark, Mariko, author. | Eleanor, Rachel, illustrator.
Title: The book of belonging : Bible stories for kind and contemplative kids /
written by Mariko Clark ; illustrated by Rachel Eleanor.
Description: First edition. | New York : Convergent Books, an imprint of Random House,
a division of Penguin Random House LLC, [2024] | Includes bibliographical references.
Identifiers: LCCN 2024000554 | ISBN 9780593580318 (hardcover ; acid-free paper) |
ISBN 9780593580325 (ebook)
Subjects: LCSH: Bible stories, English—Juvenile literature. |
Bible—Paraphrases—Juvenile literature.
Classification: LCC BS550.3 .C547 2024 | DDC 220.95/05—dc23/eng/20240226
LC record available at https://lccn.loc.gov/2024000554

Printed in China

convergentbooks.com

10 9 8 7 6 5 4 3 2 1

First Edition

Book design by Marysarah Quinn and Lynne Yeamans
Cover design by Rachel Eleanor and Lynne Yeamans

For Aidah Hope

This book exists because you ask big questions.
Please don't ever stop.

—MC

For Finn

I started making these pictures before I even met
you, imagining the world I wanted to gift to you. And
then you grew inside me as I grew this book. This
world isn't quite as kind or safe as I'd like, but I want
you to know that your mommy tried hard to make it
better not only for you but also for other kids and their
grown-ups, and most especially for the in-betweeners,
lost sheep, and wandering ones. We all belong.

—RE

CONTENTS

NEW TESTAMENT {159}

INTRODUCTION

 HIS IS A BOOK INSPIRED BY STORIES FROM THE BIBLE. And what is the Bible? The Bible is a very old, very long book, made up of many different types of stories. Some of the stories are told through poems and songs, some are more like history lessons, some are official royal records, and some are letters.

But they all work together to teach us what God is like. What is God like? Well, that is a big question with many lovely, complicated answers—answers that you will likely spend the rest of your life exploring, because most of the time, these stories don't just come right out and give us the answers. (That would be much easier.) Often they show more than they tell.

And they present to us who God is through the history of God's family: people who were learning to trust God in the middle of their messy lives. They learned bits and pieces of who God is and they saved their stories for us to learn from. But God is too big to fit into even our most imaginative human words, so all throughout history, people who have tried to describe God say things like "God protects us like a mother bird sitting on her nest." Or "God is everywhere, like the wind." Or "God comforts us, like a hug." We've tried to display that too, in our different illustrations of God.

We've imagined God with a face that frowns and smiles, with arms that help and hold, with a mouth to breathe and speak. In some stories, God is shown looking like a hovering bird, a covering cloud, or a bright-

ening fire. But it's important to remember that we don't know what God looks like. We only know what God *is* like. So each picture is a beautiful, true idea for our eyes to rest on while our hearts do the important work of learning to trust God's big, mysterious fullness.

One of the most special things about learning stories from the Bible is that they teach us about who we are. We get to learn the names God has for us, the people God made. The more we read the Bible, the more names we will learn. There are three big names that seem really special to God, three that show up again and again in the stories we've shared here:

BELONGING

BELOVED

DELIGHTFUL

BELONGING

Is there anything more cozy than the feeling of belonging? A place especially for you that no one else could ever fill? Sometimes we feel it in our families or with our friends. Sometimes we feel it on our birthday or when we climb our favorite tree. The Bible is filled with stories of God telling God's people, "You belong with me!" No matter how lost or lonesome we feel, there is always a place for us with God.

BELOVED

Love is the most powerful force in the universe. It is bigger and deeper and truer and brighter than we can understand.

Beloved is really just a fancy way to say, "Someone Who Is Loved." Someone who is loved so thoroughly that it becomes who they are. It becomes their name.

Here's something pretty amazing: God loves people so much that God says each and every one of us should have this name. Beloved Me, Beloved You, Beloved Us. We are all Beloved.

DELIGHTFUL

You make God happy, just by being you. Before we did anything or said anything, God was delighted with us. But we often forget, and it trips us up! So the Bible is full of stories of God reminding people that they don't need to earn God's delight or hide when they make mistakes. They just have to trust God says that they Belong, they are Beloved, and they are Delightful.

And while we're talking about names, you will notice that the names I've used in stories you are familiar with may look different. Mary is Miryam. John is Yokhanan. That's because I've decided to include the original names for these characters as they would have been known to the Bible writers and its original readers and to many people today around the world who speak Hebrew and Greek.

One way to think about Bible reading is that the Bible can be a mirror and also a window. Like a mirror, the Bible should help us see ourselves. Just like the characters in the stories, we can follow God and learn to trust the names God calls us. But the Bible should also be a window, helping us see into an ancient Middle Eastern world that is probably very different from our own. By noting the original names, I hope to honor the people and traditions with whom these stories originated!

Bible stories have been told and retold for thousands of years. There is so much to learn from each and every story. One of the most special things about the Bible is that we can learn something new and true from each retelling. Wise teachers have said it's as though people who love God take turns holding a big, beautiful gemstone. With each retelling, they turn it and we see God's light sparkle through in a new and different way.

Whatever you learn from the way the gem turns in these stories, the biggest treasure I hope you find is this: God is trustworthy, and God's names for you are true. You Belong. You are Beloved. You are Delightful.

OLD TESTAMENT

A VERY GOOD SONG

GENESIS 1-2

Khavah is also called Eve.

 T FIRST, THERE WAS A SWIRLING, watery mess. It was somehow chaotic and empty, all at the same time. It was everything and nothing at once.

But God began to speak, and God's Spirit hovered over the mess like a mother bird over her nest. Or maybe it was more like a deep breath one takes before launching into song or like a wind that ushers in springtime. None of our words seem quite marvelous enough to describe what God's Spirit was doing.

God sang a love song, and life emerged.

God took the mess and made it meaningful.

God took the emptiness and filled it with goodness.

First, God made light and it blazed to life. And God's Spirit clapped with delight as God separated the light from the darkness. "This is ready. This is *good*," God decided and went about the holy work of naming, telling the new creations who they are and who they belong to. "You will be called Day. You will be called Night."

Next, God spread out the sky, and it was just as much fun, with all the making and the delight and the naming. God gathered up the water and made room for land. ("Good!" "Your name is Land!" "And you are Sea.") And God filled the land with every kind of plant and tree that you could imagine.

It was as if God popped the top right off of God's imagination and then whatever danced to life was loved, delighted in, and named. All things bright and beautiful sang and spun into place.

The sun! The moon!
Stars and planets!

Good! Good! Good!

Flopping fish to
fill the seas!

Flapping birds to fill the skies!

Flocks and herds to fill the land!
Swarming and teeming,
spilling and tumbling!
Good! Good! Good!
Good! Good!

Where there was once an echoing mess, there was now a symphony of sights and sounds. All the jolly jumble of a very fine party. But God wasn't done yet—there were a few guests missing.

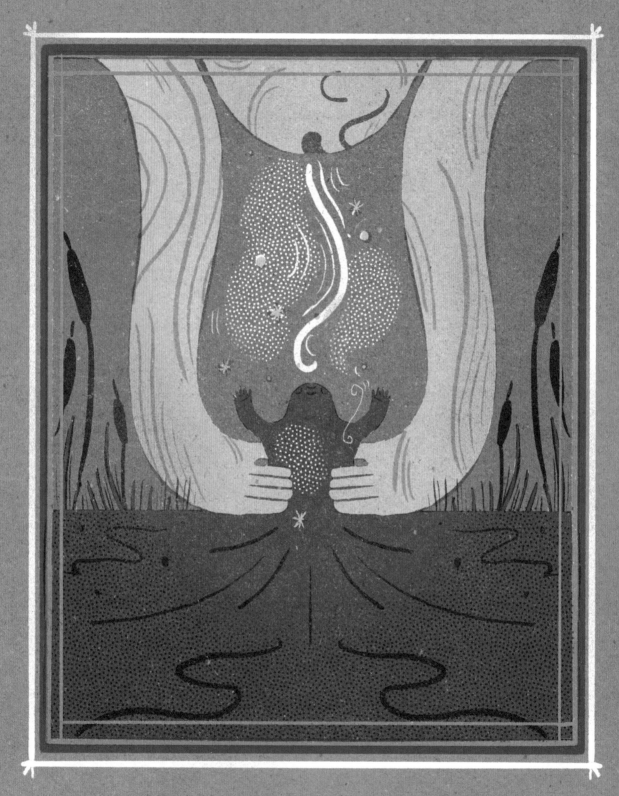

God made humans next: Khavah (Eve) and Adam. God formed them from the rich red-brown earth and filled them with God's Spirit so they would be like God. They would create and delight and name, just like God. They would care for the plants and seas and animals—all things bright and beautiful. "*Very* good," God said, like an artist examining their master-piece. Or maybe it was like the way a bird considers the nest it has built. Or maybe it was like the way a parent marvels at their newborn baby.

None of our words seem quite tender enough to describe God's delight as God looked at the humans.

They're beautiful! They're ready! They're just as they should be.

I like them and I love them.

They're GOOD.

After all the creating and delighting and naming, God rested. And God called this resting time Sabbath and declared that it should be celebrated like a little holiday at the end of every week—a reminder of what God did

after God made us. Like a mama who snuggles up to enjoy her baby after giving birth, looking over its little ears and tiny fingernails, God stopped and *enjoyed* the good, good creation. It was as it should be—nothing left to do but be together. And just as you will never stop being your mama's baby, no matter how big you get, God's people will always belong with God. No matter what.

God had a dream of togetherness in
a world where everything matches the
good, good goodness of God. And guess
what? Even though God had finished
and creation was ready, the enjoyment
was just beginning. In fact, God is still
enjoying God's good, good creation
and inviting you to enjoy it too.

You belong with God.
You are loved by God.
And you are very good.

WONDER MOMENT

PEOPLE WHO LOVE GOD BELIEVE *SO* MANY DIFFERENT things about Bible stories, especially this one!

Who wrote down the story? Did God write the story or did people? Is it somehow both? Did this really happen, or is it a beautiful poem of wonderings? Is it somehow both? Was it seven actual days, or seven long seasons? How many species were created?

So many wonderful questions! And guess who loves questions? God!

Think about how cozy and special you feel when someone asks you about your day or wants to learn more about your favorite foods or hobbies. God made us to belong with God! That means God wants to be close and cozy with us. So *all* questions are welcome!

Hopefully, you will spend your whole life asking important questions about God. Sometimes there will be easy answers. Sometimes you will decide on one thing and change your mind as you learn more. And sometimes you get to giggle and throw your hands up and decide, *That is something only God could understand!*

Here is what we do know: Bible stories were written a very, very long time ago. Long before most of the science we use today. Long before most of the history we have today. The people who wrote these stories wanted us to know God. So although we get to wonder and giggle and chat about so many questions, the most important one is this:

What does this story teach us about God?

THE GARDEN OF FORGOTTEN NAMES

GENESIS 2-3

Khavah is also called Eve.

OD PLANTED A SPECTACULAR GARDEN WHERE Khavah (Eve) and Adam would live and work. A safe and lovely place of belonging. You see, God loved Eve and Adam and had a beautiful dream for them. "I made you like me, so I want you to care for the gardens and the animals just as I would," God told Eve and Adam. There was much to learn about, and what a glad time God would have, holding their hands and teaching them. Step by step, they would learn God's wisdom, which leads to a good and peaceful life.

I belong with you, and you belong with me. Come, let me show you how to live.

In the middle of their garden were two trees: the Life Tree and the Good and Bad Knowledge Tree. And God warned them, "Eat from any tree in the garden except the Good and Bad Knowledge Tree. You are not ready for that knowledge yet. It will lead to death and destruction." God knew that having so much knowledge

without learning wisdom would only hurt and harm them. God was protecting them from that harm and asking them to trust God's dream.

So there they were: God, Eve, Adam, the fish, the birds, and the animals—all together, just as they belonged, among the great, green growing things. A grand garden party indeed.

Imagine the delight in their days:

Climbing the fruit trees to gather food; flipping and swinging with the monkeys, lemurs, squirrels, and sloths; chattering at the rainbows of birds.

*Caring for the plants and
flowers as the honeybees and
butterflies danced around their heads
and as the rabbits tumbled around their
feet with the tapirs and armadillos.*

*Riding elephants, splashing into the rivers, and swimming among
the schools of fish, turtles, and platypuses.*

*Sleeping snuggled with ocelots, oryx, and capybaras as
the crickets wheedled and God's Spirit shushed among
the bulrushes.*

They all had what they needed
to live and flourish. They grew
and learned from God. And
it was good, just as God
had said. It was like a
wild, happy child-
hood from a
fairy tale.

But like most fairy tales, this story has a crisis. And it starts with a crafty, talking snake. The snake approached Eve and Adam as they frolicked through the garden, wild and naked and free. "Did God really say you couldn't eat from any tree in the garden?" the snake asked. "We eat from all the trees!" Eve replied. "Well, except the one at the center. God told us it would lead to death." The snake laughed in a way that made Eve feel very silly and small. "Death and doom? Oh, no, no, no. God is keeping things from you! The fruit won't make you die; it will make you smart like God!" said the snake. The snake was very crafty.

Crafty enough to know that you can tell a truth that's not the *whole* truth. Crafty enough to know that you can become *smart* without being wise.

Eve and Adam were faced with a choice, one we all make over and over again as we grow older and wiser: *Will I trust who God says God is and who God says I am, or will I trust other names?*

What did God say over and over again during the wondrous Creation song? *It's good! They're very good! Good, good, good. They're just as they should be!*

But you are not as you should be, the snake had suggested. *You're not smart enough! God is keeping things from you. You're not good. You don't have what you need for life and flourishing. The fruit will make you smart like God.*

Eve looked at the fruit. Somewhere in the distance, she heard the tumbling rabbits and the swinging monkeys. *Good, good. They're just as they should be.* The elephants splashed, and the ocelots stretched. *Good, good. They have everything they need.* She stood in the garden with Adam, and she reached out her hand and she chose.

Eve ate the fruit. Adam ate the fruit. They didn't trust God. They believed what the snake said more than they believed what God said. They grabbed for God's gifts, snatching at knowledge instead of trusting God to teach them. It was like pressing fast-forward on their lives. Like turning four and then forty-four. Like going to college right after kindergarten. All at once, they knew what God knows without walking with God: They missed out on the wonder of learning and living! Imagine the weight of their world.

Suddenly their precious garden home looked different. They saw the

sharp teeth of their animal friends, the laughing sneer of the crafty snake, and their thoughts raced with worry. *They* looked different. They now felt silly being naked all the time and hurried to cover up the amazing bodies God created and called good.

God came walking through the garden and called out, "You belong with me. Why aren't you with me?"

"I was hiding from you. I trembled because I was naked," said Adam in a small voice.

"Oh, my beloved children. Who told you that you were naked?" God asked. "Did you eat from the one tree I told you to stay away from?"

Adam pointed to Eve, who pointed to the snake. "We were tricked!"

"Things will be different now," God told them, lifting up their tiny faces. God knew that with knowledge would come choices. And what happened that day would happen again: Eve and Adam would choose to trust untrue names. They would forget that God said, "You are Beloved, you are Delightful, and you Belong!" That forgetting would bring pain, confusion, and destruction—the opposite of God's dream for them!

But God created people to belong with God, and they always will. Places of belonging will always exist. Places where heaven touches earth. Places for humans to meet with God. "Nothing can stop my love for you, my dream for you," God was reminding Eve and Adam.

Just as the olive trees keep making olives, which contain the seed to more trees, which make more olives in an everlasting cycle; just as the elephants, the birds, the ocelot, and the oryx all birth young who grow up to birth more young

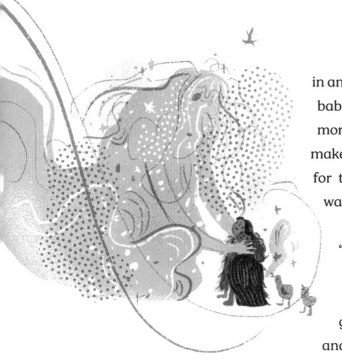

in an everlasting cycle; Eve would have babies who would grow up to make more babies who would grow up to make more babies. Parents would care for those babies and teach them to walk close to God.

"Someday," God promised them, "one of those babies will be the place where heaven meets earth once and for all. That baby will grow up to silence untrue voices and untrue names that convince you not to trust me. He will show you how to live with knowledge *and* wisdom. He will make all things new."

It was time to go. God sent Eve and Adam out from the garden. They were made from the earth and filled with God's breath, which would always twist and tug inside them. They would grasp for goodness and beg for blessing. They would soar and stumble, but they would never be alone. They would learn wisdom by walking with God in the wide and wild world.

MINDFUL MOMENT

EVE AND ADAM TRUSTED THE UNTRUE NAMES THAT THE snake suggested more than they trusted God's good names for them. It seems to be part of our humanness to sometimes trust untrue names. And what we believe about who we are matters! It changes the way we act. That is why it's so important to know and trust God's names for us.

Learning to trust God takes time. We need to learn who God is and what God's voice sounds like and what God's Spirit feels like. Throughout this whole book, you will learn many different names for God and many different names that God calls *you*. Let's remember some of those names!

Close your eyes and take some deep belly breaths. Then put your hand over your heart like you're pressing on a name tag. Repeat these names:

I am Loved.   *I am Treasured.*

I Belong with God.   *I am Honored.*

I am Good.   *I am Never Alone.*

I am Purposed.   *I am Protected.*

We learn to trust these names as we grow to know and trust God. And who is God? Well, that is something we spend our whole lives learning. God is so big and wonderful that none of our words can quite describe God. But here are some names that describe parts of God: Creator, Gracious, Merciful, Patient, Loving Father, Good Shepherd, Helper, Strong Tower, Mother Hen, Gentle Dove, Birthing Mama, Peace, Rescuer.

GOD'S DREAM

OD WAS RIGHT, OF COURSE. EVE AND ADAM HAD children and grandchildren and great-grandchildren. Each person born into the wide and wild world had to make choices: *Is God trustworthy? Do I trust God's names for me?*

Sometimes they trusted God's names and lived as people safe in their Belonging, Belovedness, and Delightfulness. Sometimes they made wise choices. They were gracious and patient. They cared for the earth and one another. There was love and life and flourishing. As you can imagine, those times looked a lot like God's dream. But that wasn't always the case.

Sometimes they trusted untrue names, believing they were Unlovable, Alone, Bad. Sometimes they acted cruelly and competitively, fighting for their belonging. They acted scared and ashamed, trying to earn love or put on a show to make others like them.

Like camels who grew weary, lying down beside the path they should travel. Like an arrow that misses its target. Like a tree that grows crooked in a harsh and rocky habitat. Like a traveler who wanders off the path. God's people sinned; they made mistakes. But no matter what they did, God knew their true names. No matter what they did, God's dream never changed:

I belong with you, and you belong with me.
Nothing can stop my love.
I will love you when you turn away from me.
I will love you when you hurt one another.
I will love you when you harm the earth.
I will love you when you
believe untrue names for yourself.
I will love you when you believe untrue names for me.
And I will love you when you forget me.

This was important, because we often forget, don't we? But God never does.

A FAMILY OF BELONGING

GENESIS 12-15

Sarai is also called Sarah. Avraham is also called Abraham.

UST AND STARLIGHT. STARLIGHT AND DUST. SARAI (Sarah) and Avraham (Abraham) had been traveling across long and lonesome stretches of land, hemmed in by the dust below and the stars above.

Have you ever noticed how long walks help straighten out your thoughts? *Left, right, left, right.* Something about the plodding rhythm

settles things into place. Abraham had been walking for so long that all his thoughts lay smooth. Smooth as the starry sky. Smooth as the dusty road. *God knows me,* Abraham thought. He had untangled that in the first few hours of walking. *God spoke to me.* He remembered it clearly, like an echo in his head. *God made big promises.*

God had asked Abraham to pack up his life and travel to a brand-new land. "Follow me to a new land, where I will make your family grow into a nation," was God's invitation. "From that new land, through your great family, I will bless the whole world." God's dream for people had not changed. They were made to belong with and be like God—to care for the earth and one another. Abraham and Sarah were being invited to join that dream. To start a new place of belonging, where everyone could learn about God and God's good names for them.

So they followed God to the Promised Land. Sarah and Abraham had many miles to mull over God's promises, but there was one they returned to when the road felt long. *A family. A family of our own. Could it be?*

Abraham and Sarah were old—as old as your great-grandparents—yet they had never been able to have children. The promise of a family kept the two of them walking, through starlight and dust, toward God's dream. But their hearts held questions. As time went by and Abraham's family stayed small, his trust began to tremble. But God was still with them. Reliable, merciful, and always kind. "Don't be afraid, Abraham," God soothed. "You're protected, and you're never alone. I will bless you."

"But when? How?" Abraham pleaded, his hope now a mere whisper.

"We've been following you for so very long, yet we still don't have children." He stood under the night sky, feeling very small and forgotten.

"Look up," came the voice of God, fresh and familiar as the wind. "See if you can count the stars, from here to the horizon. That's how big your family will be." Abraham's head tipped back, and his eyes grew round with wonder. He could count all night and still never finish! *This is how many family members God is promising? How can this be? How can it not be?*

The God who made the stars, named the night, and called the whole earth good was the same God who made Sarah's womb, watching over its emptiness and ache. "Look down," God said next. Abraham watched the dust dance and settle in the cool night air. "Your family will be like the dust of the earth: impossible to count." Like his ancestors before him, stretching back for generations, Abraham was being asked by God to trust. *But is God trustworthy?* That was the age-old question.

As Abraham stood, bathed in starlight and dust, he considered his journey with God to this new place. His travels with Sarah had been long and their mistakes many, but God had always been with them. When they stumbled, God had scooped them up. When they failed, God had been faithful. When they were in danger, God had delivered them.

"Okay," Abraham finally replied as the crags and folds of his weather-worn face rose up into a smile. Throwing his hands up in a gesture both exhausted and amused, he sighed and said, "I trust you." Abraham's circumstances shifted like dust, and his hopes flickered in and out like the stars. But God was a solid place to belong. Abraham rested in that belonging and trusted in God's dream. It was exactly right, exactly good, exactly as it should be.

SHE LAUGHED

GENESIS 18

Sarai is also called Sarah. Avraham is also called Abraham.
Yishmael is also called Ishmael. Yitzhak is also called Isaac.

WEAT DRIPPED FROM THE WOMEN'S FACES AS THEY hurried around the tent, baking and stirring and scooping. Every once in a while, they stopped to glower at each other. Silver-haired Sarai (Sarah) was hunched in bitterness. The younger woman, called Hagar, was stiff with protectiveness. "Hurry up with that bread, Hagar," said Sarah, breaking the silence. The younger woman kneaded quietly, screaming in her mind. *Slice! Stir! Scoop! Sizzle!*

There was no time to untangle the feelings, because three strangers had arrived at their camp that morning, and the women were busy preparing a welcome meal. *Slice! Stir! Scoop!* The two women worked in

sizzling silence, so many sharp words unsaid between them.

Sarah had not always been this way, sharp and biting. The Sarah that had followed Avraham (Abraham) from their homeland into a new adventure had been soft and hopeful. *A family. A family of our own!* she had marveled, full of anticipation. But a year passed, then five, then ten, and God's good promises started to feel like a distant, teasing dream. Despair is easier than hope, control is easier than trust, so Sarah grasped for God's gifts with a harmful plan of her own: "You might as well marry Hagar! Start this new family with her!" she had shouted when she shoved the young woman toward Abraham.

Oh, the fear, the doubts, the untrue names Sarah had trusted. They

rippled out in hurt and harm as she found a way to reach for the family she wanted. Her plan worked—sort of. Abraham's new wife had a son. They named him Yishmael (Ishmael) and loved him dearly. But Sarah was left on the outside, watching their family form. *Slice! Stir! Scoop!*

As the women worked, the voice of one of their visitors floated through the tent flap from where they sat outside with Abraham. "Where is your wife Sarah?" one of them asked. *I'm here, alone. The outsider in my own home yet again,* Sarah thought. Her glare cut to the younger woman and then to Ishmael beside her. Sarah peeked through the tent flap at Abraham. *Your God promised us a great family,* she thought. *We left our home, our friends, everyone we know. Yet here I am, alone and empty.*

Slice! Stir! Sizzle!

And it was as if her hurting heart beat loud enough to be heard outside, because another voice floated into the tent just then, saying, "I'll return next year and your wife Sarah will have a son!" Sarah froze, silver and silent. *A son? Me? After all this time?* She looked down at her body, aging and empty. She looked over at the younger woman and the son they never spoke of. *Now I get my own baby? Now?*

And she couldn't help it—she laughed, sharp and bitter. But God knew everything Sarah's laugh held: disbelief, despair, and a feeble hope. "Why did you laugh? Is anything too marvelous for me?" came God's voice. Was it a challenge? Was it a comfort? Sarah felt both as she wrestled with God's words. But as sure as starlight and as constant as dust, God was right, of course. Sarah finally became pregnant, even in her old age. But as her belly grew, fear and mistrust battled with her joy.

Is this too good to be true?

Is God tricking me?

Will I finally feel less lonesome?

The year drew to a close, and Sarah gave birth to her son. They named him Yitzhak (Isaac), which means laughter. And this time, Sarah's laugh was light and soft as she gazed at her special baby. She had journeyed so far, waited so long. She had wrestled and stumbled and shouted and grieved. She had trusted many names, but on this one she and God agreed: Sarah was a mother.

5

THE GOD WHO SEES

GENESIS 16; 21

Yishmael is also called Ishmael. Yitzhak is also called Isaac.
Sarai is also called Sarah. Avraham is also called Abraham.

HE YOUNG WOMAN GRIPPED HER SON'S HAND AND staggered across the sand. With every sinking step, her heavy heart sank too. *I just want to go home. I miss my family. I just want to belong again.*

She squinted against the setting sun and imagined the welcome they'd receive when they got back to Egypt. How good it would be to smell her native dishes, to feel her mother's hug, to hear her true name spoken. *They took away my name,* she'd sob into her mother's shoulder. *They just call me Hagar.*

The alien.

The foreign one. The stranger.

She had been gone for many years, enslaved in Sarai's (Sarah's) tent. So much had happened.

Even though God chose Sarah and Avraham (Abraham) to start God's great family of belonging, they forgot God's promises. Instead of waiting, they tried to grab what God was giving.

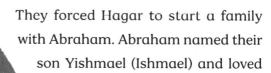

They forced Hagar to start a family with Abraham. Abraham named their son Yishmael (Ishmael) and loved him dearly. But then God's promise to Sarah was at last fulfilled. Sarah had a baby of her own and named him Yitzhak (Isaac). Two sons, one promise. When Isaac and Ishmael were old enough to argue, Sarah saw what the future would be. So once again, she grabbed for God's gifts by sending Hagar and Ishmael away.

"Get rid of that slave woman and her son! That woman's son will never share in Isaac's inheritance!" Sarah's shout still rang in Hagar's and Ishmael's ears as they stumbled through the sand. They felt unnamed, unnecessary, unwanted. God's family of belonging had cast out one of their own.

They trudged for days through the wilderness toward Egypt. The food and water ran out. The young woman's strength and hope wore thin. Finally, she laid Ishmael in the shade of a small bush, weeping as she noticed his cracked lips and shallow breaths. Stumbling a few feet away, she felt despair pull her to the ground. She heard Ishmael crying weakly

and felt her chest fill with fear and sorrow. *We just want to go home,* she thought.

"Don't be afraid," came a voice from heaven, cool and refreshing on her wind-worn skin. "I hear Ishmael crying," the voice continued. "I see you have been crushed by cruelty and injustice. But I'm with you. Go, lift up your son and hold him close. I have big plans for him." God spoke true and beautiful names over the woman and her son, promising them hope and abundance. "I didn't bring you here to die. I brought you here to live freely. Ishmael is not doomed or forgotten! He will

EL ROI, the GOD WHO SEES ME

build his own family of belonging, with many descendants. He will be noble and free like the wild donkeys that roam the desert."

And it was exactly what the mother needed to hear for her son. It was exactly what she needed to hear for herself. After years of feeling unnamed and forgotten, here was her belonging.

God showed her a well, and she rushed to fetch a drink for Ishmael, sobbing with relief.

She turned to God and spoke true and beautiful words back: "And your name is El Roi: the God Who Sees Me. I've seen the God Who Sees Me. They took away my name, but you remembered me. I was enslaved, but now I am free."

And God did see her. God was with her and Ishmael as the boy grew up. They settled in the wilderness and created their own family of belonging.

A MIDNIGHT WRESTLING MATCH

GENESIS 32

Yaakov is also called Jacob. Avraham is also called Abraham.
Yitzhak is also called Isaac. Yisrael is also called Israel.

GRRRR!

OOF!" YAAKOV'S (JACOB'S) BREATH came out in a grunt as the stranger's knee sunk into his belly. *Is this a dream?* Jacob had been wrestling with this mysterious person all night. Exhausted and filthy, Jacob shook his head. Surely, if this were a dream, he would have woken up by now.

He dipped and dodged, trying to recall how he got there. The last thing he remembered was being on the run yet again, sending his family across the river and sitting down alone to think.

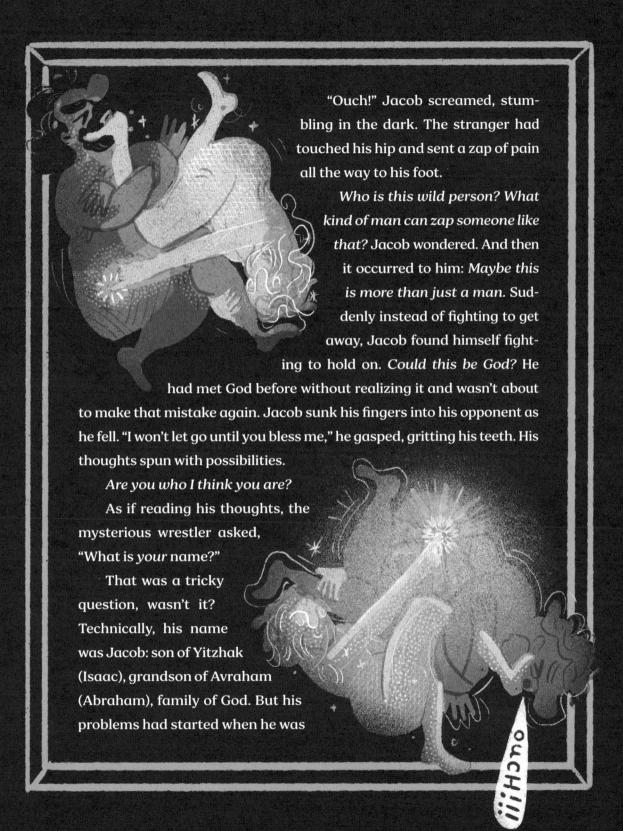

"Ouch!" Jacob screamed, stumbling in the dark. The stranger had touched his hip and sent a zap of pain all the way to his foot.

Who is this wild person? What kind of man can zap someone like that? Jacob wondered. And then it occurred to him: *Maybe this is more than just a man.* Suddenly instead of fighting to get away, Jacob found himself fighting to hold on. *Could this be God?* He had met God before without realizing it and wasn't about to make that mistake again. Jacob sunk his fingers into his opponent as he fell. "I won't let go until you bless me," he gasped, gritting his teeth. His thoughts spun with possibilities.

Are you who I think you are?

As if reading his thoughts, the mysterious wrestler asked, "What is *your* name?"

That was a tricky question, wasn't it? Technically, his name was Jacob: son of Yitzhak (Isaac), grandson of Avraham (Abraham), family of God. But his problems had started when he was

OUCH!!!

pretending to be someone else. Disguised as his brother, he had lied to his father, stealing from them both.

Impatient and insecure, Jacob had always grasped for good gifts, but it hadn't made him feel happy or safe. He was always running, always restless. Striving and struggling, desperate to belong. But if this stranger *was* God, Jacob's story was no secret. So Jacob told the truth, for the first time in a long time. "My name is Jacob."

"Very good!" God laughed. Because, of course, the mysterious wrestler was God! "And here's your blessing: From now on, your name is Yisrael

(Israel). It means 'to wrestle.' You and your children and your children's children will go by this name. I'm inviting you to a wrestling match. Hold on to me! I'll squirm; you'll swerve. We will be close and then far away. At times it will be fun, and our joy will spill right over. At times it will hurt, but you'll get stronger and smarter because I won't let you go! I'll always be right here. Get mad, get sad, get tired—I'm not scared of your feelings! I love to wrestle, and I'll keep chasing you.

"You don't need to cheat your way into love, and you don't need to run scared. Just hold on to me."

"And what is your name?" Jacob couldn't help but ask his wrestling partner. He thought he knew, but he had to be sure!

Yet the only answer he got was, "Why do you ask my name?" And with that, God was gone.

As the sun rose over the land, melting like butter across the sand, Jacob found himself alone again. He sat by the stream, staring at his rippling reflection. *Hello, Israel.* He had begged for a blessing. A true name. A place to belong. And God—*Was it God? It must have been God*—had invited him to take his restless, striving ways and spend a lifetime wrestling together. *Just hold on to me.* He considered the brother he had tricked, the father he had lied to, and the people he had used and escaped. He decided to make things right. To wrestle for goodness instead of running away.

Standing to leave, Jacob—now called Israel—stumbled. "Ow!" His hip screamed with pain, shooting all the way to his foot. Yet he smiled as he limped along, carrying the story of his new name with every step.

MINDFUL MOMENT

JACOB'S LIMP TOLD THE STORY OF HIS LIFE-CHANGING encounter with God. How do you think he felt, sharing the story with others?

Every body is different, and every body tells a story. Your body has stories, and so do the bodies of people around you.

Stories about scars on knees.
Stories about tubes in tummies.
Stories about freckles on noses.
Stories about devices in ears.
Stories about hair that is long and hair that is gone.

Sharing our stories is part of the way we wrestle with God, so let's practice! Starting at the tippy top of your head, let your focus travel down your wonderful body, telling stories along the way. (For example, "There are freckles on my nose because I love to play outside!") You can tell them to yourself or to a loved one.

For every story you tell, finish with this: "And that's the story of my _____. It is good because God made it!"

THE GREAT BABY RESCUE

EXODUS 1–2

Yokheved is also called Jochebed. Miryam is also called Miriam.
Moshe is also called Moses. Tziporah is also called Zipporah.
Hebrew is another word for Abraham's descendants.

HE IBIS STRETCHED THEIR WINGS WHILE THE crocodiles lounged, plump and smug on the banks of the Nile River. It was almost harvest season in Egypt, and everything was green, glossy, and growing, growing,

growing. God's family was growing too. They had come to Egypt many generations before and flourished, like everything seemed to, in the rich, black soil, growing into the great family God had promised Avraham (Abraham) so long ago.

But things began to change. There was a new king (called Pharaoh) who was threatened by the flourishing of God's family. He enslaved them: miserable work, no pay, lugging heavy bricks in the hot Egyptian sun. Where they used to be special guests, now they were treated as bodies to be beaten into obedience. They were tools in Pharaoh's kingdom, which loomed like a great power machine fueled by sweat, blood, agony, and groans.

Just when God's people thought things couldn't get worse, fearful Pharaoh shocked them all. Desperate to stop God's family from growing, growing, growing, he announced a plan to get rid of all their newborn babies. God's people felt tears, terror, and then a rush of protective fury. Pharaoh should know better than to threaten beloved babies. Mothers and fathers, aunts, friends, and siblings—God's people wailed, and God put a rescue plan into motion.

All that was needed was a team of cunning, courageous women.

Puah and Shifrah, midwives to God's people, were busy day and night, helping pregnant moms bring their babies into the world. The work of welcoming life brings a person close to the Creator, and these women knew that every baby was sacred. So when Pharaoh summoned

them with his decree of destruction, they refused. Life and flourishing, they insisted. And God blessed them. But Pharaoh was furious.

A new mom named Yokheved (Jochebed) studied her son, fretting over Pharaoh's fury. *How long can I keep him secret? Will he ever be truly safe?* She placed him in a basket with a sob and a kiss and set it at the edge of the river. *Life and flourishing,* she prayed over and over, sending his older sister, Miryam (Miriam), to watch over him from shore.

"What's that?" Pharaoh's daughter tiptoed into the river to bathe and spotted the basket among the green and glossy plants. When a wail and a wiggle confirmed that this was no ordinary discovery, her heart softened. "I'll call him Moshe (Moses)!" she said, snuggling and soothing the baby, who was hungry from all his travels.

"I know someone who can help feed him!" Watchful Miriam spoke up from the riverbank. She was thinking of her own mother. So Pharaoh's daughter hired Jochebed to feed her own baby.

Years passed. The Nile swelled and receded. Just as its waters brought life and carved new shapes in the shoreline, so Moses was growing, growing, growing—nourished and molded by his mothers. A trickle of sacrifice from his birth mother's surrender. A splash of courage from his midwives. A swirling eddy of empathy from his adoptive mother. Deep wells of intelligence and action from his wise and watchful sister.

And so this Hebrew baby, hunted by Pharaoh, saved and shaped by women, grew to be an Egyptian prince. From the palace Moses called

home, Pharaoh's power machine surged on, built upon the backs of Moses's people.

This kingdom, with all its riches, could belong to Moses next. But did he want it? Torn and tortured by these two worlds, Moses fled to the wilderness. *Where do I belong?* he wondered. And then, when his future seemed murky, he was rescued again, for there, by a wilderness well, Moses met and married Tziporah (Zipporah), a shepherd who showed him a new and gentle way to wield power.

And so it was that God's team of ordinary extraordinary women pulled off the great baby rescue. And their courage flowed one to the next, swelling and expanding like the mighty Nile to deliver into destiny a deliverer named Moses.

THE PEOPLE GOD GOES WITH

EXODUS 3-14

Moshe is also called Moses. Aharon is also called Aaron.

OSHE (MOSES) AMBLED ALONG THROUGH THE LOW shrubs and tumbling rocks, following his flock and listening to the mountain wind yawn. Wandering left him plenty of time alone with his thoughts: *Who am I? Am I Egyptian? Am I Hebrew? Am I enslaved? Am I an enslaver? Does it even matter?*

He was a long way from home. This made him feel free but also very much alone and unnamed. Born to a Hebrew mother, raised in the Egyptian palace, hiding out in the country after getting into trouble with both groups, Moses found himself in a lonely and deserted place. As he glanced to his left, Moses noticed something strange in the distance: a lone bush, completely aflame. As he approached, a voice came from the bush, as warm and commanding as the purr of a great lion. "Moses, Moses."

"Here I am," replied Moses, awestruck.

"I am the God your ancestors knew," the voice continued. "It's time we met as well. I've heard the groans of my people in Egypt. I see how they suffer. I've come to rescue them and lead them back to the Promised Land. And I'm sending you to Pharaoh to bring them there from Egypt."

Moses sputtered, wide-eyed, "Me? Why would you choose me—of all people—for such a task?"

And the mysterious voice seemed to smile as it responded, "I am with you."

That's not what I asked, Moses thought. He narrowed his eyes and whispered, "Who are you?"

"I am who I am," came the puzzling reply. "You'll see what and who I am by how I act." God's voice resembled a warm wind, soothing yet adventuresome. "I love you because I am love. I save you because I am safe. I comfort you because I am comfort. I am with you because I am here."

"You're asking me to speak to the people of Israel, but haven't you noticed that I stutter?" Moses protested. Sometimes his mouth had trouble forming words. Sometimes they felt stuck behind his tongue and all he could do was make noise.

"Who do you think made your mouth, Moses? It was me. Whether or not you think it works well, I'll be with you. I'll be with your mouth."

Moses begged God to send someone else. And even though God believed in Moses more than Moses did, God offered to send his brother, Aharon (Aaron), with him to help him speak. "I'll be with you, and I'll be with Aaron. Pharaoh has terrorized my people for far too long. And though he is treated as a god among the many gods of Egypt, he is just a man. A cruel man. A bully. But I am bigger than any bully, and soon everyone will see that. I will show them through many wonders."

Moses traveled all the way back to Egypt and told the family of God, "God hears you, sees you, and wants to rescue you

ENOUGH!

and be close to you." And the people believed him and trusted God. *We are not alone. God has come to rescue us.*

But just as God warned, Pharaoh clung to his power. He wasn't willing to give up the enslaved people—the key to his power machine. But God displayed how God was bigger than Pharaoh and all his gods by sending many wonders and troubles—bugs and frogs and boils and hail—until everyone stood in awe of the power of God's love. Finally, Pharaoh said, "Enough! Take your people and your flocks and your herds and be gone! Go and be with your God."

And so God's people, enslaved for more than four hundred years, stood and followed God out of that land of heartache and horror. They shook off the names that Pharaoh had called them—Slave, Forgotten, Throwaway—and trusted in a new name: the People God Goes With.

BE GONE!

A PATH TO FREEDOM

 RAPPED. THERE WAS NO WAY AROUND IT. Pharaoh had changed his mind, chasing after God's people. And now with a great shimmering sea to their front and a pack of angry Pharaoh-soldiers fast approaching from behind, God's people were trapped. Stuck. Doomed.

Babies wailed, and old men grumbled as everyone turned their frightened eyes to Moses. *What now?* "Be calm! God will make a way!" Moses assured them. *Hello? God? Will you make a way?*

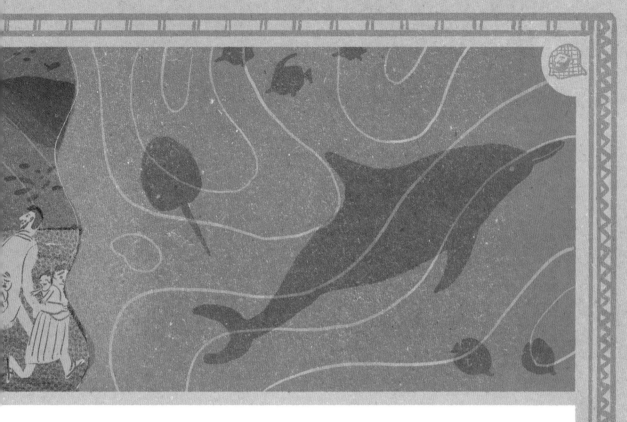

"Lift up your staff and stretch your hand over the water," God told Moses. Moses looked down at the shepherd staff that he had chosen over Pharaoh's crook. God had asked him to stand for life and flourishing instead of power. God had promised to go with him. It all came down to this: A shepherd against a pharaoh. God against Egypt. Staff versus crook. Flourishing versus power.

As Moses lifted the staff, a mighty wind blew, and the waters rolled back, splashing and piling into walls on either side. A path appeared—a way through the water. Tiptoeing, dust-kicking, jaws dropping, God's people crossed the mighty sea on dry land. And as soon as the last foot climbed the opposite bank, the waters folded back in with a crash! The chase was over. Pharaoh had lost. God's people were free.

THE SONG OF THE SEA

EXODUS 15

Miryam is also called Miriam.

 SIGH OF RELIEF PASSED THROUGH THE PEOPLE God Goes With, burbling into a giggle as it went, until they were all laughing, crying, and hugging. You know that sad-happy startle you feel when waking from a bad dream? Yup, it was kind of like that. They were safe. They were free. Free at last. God's promises are good.

They crowded together on the seashore. The same sea they had just walked through. They *had* walked through it, hadn't they? It was hard to believe but impossible to deny.

As the feelings flowed through them, people began to move and make noise. A victory kick: *Yah, yah.* A wail of wonder: *Wooooowwwweeee!* A stomp of homesickness: *Stomp, stomp.* A shrug of grief. A wiggle of anticipation. A clap of praise.

Miryam (Miriam) stood still for a long moment, remembering another escape through other waters not so long ago. The fear and hope that had hammered in her chest as she followed her baby brother in the basket were even louder now after following him through the sea. Fear, hope: *Tum tum tum.*

Then, as bold and decisive as she had been as a girl, she took up her hand drum and began to play, matching the thumping of her heart. Fear, hope: *Tum tum tum.* The other women grinned and joined her, and soon the whole family of God was moving with loud, gleeful worship as Miriam sang out,

Sing to God, a shout of victory! In the darkest night,
God rescued me.

God is the strength in my legs, the song in my mouth.

God is my rescuer. This is a beautiful God,
who makes beautiful things!

Our parents taught us to trust God, and we
weren't let down!

The one who fights for us is here with us.

God defeats every lie and speaks truth over me!

My fears, my tormentors, those who harmed and insulted me—
God has defeated them. They will never hurt me again.

God's hands saved us. God's hands hold us.
God's hands soothe us.

Who is like you, God, a mighty Spirit?

Who is like you, God, both holy and near?

You lead us with your love.
You guide us with your strong kindness.

You welcome us home.

You know where we belong, because we belong with you.

You will bring us to a peaceful place,
a place where you dwell forever.

And so God's people started their new lives with free and ferocious dancing. The people Pharaoh had used and discarded, named Worthless and Disposable, now shimmered in their freedom. *Yah, yah! Wooowwwweee! Stomp, stomp. Tum tum tum.* God saw them, named them, rescued them, and claimed them.

MERCY AND MANNA

EXODUS 16

Moshe is also called Moses.

HOUGH THE ROAD FROM EGYPT TO THE PROMISED
Land was short and straight, it passed by fierce and unfamiliar tribes. God's people were still shaking and worried from
the horrors of Egypt. So, like a loving parent soothes a frightened child by cuddling them in a quiet room, God led the people off the
road, into the windswept wilderness. A land of sunbaked stillness where
listening comes easier. A place to rest, feel safe, and get to know God. And
there, away from distraction and danger, God reminded them, "I belong
with you, and you belong with me. You're my beloved. I'll care for you."

But trust takes time, and as their provisions from Egypt ran low,
the people soon began to worry and complain. "God brought us to the
wilderness to starve!" they groaned.

Endlessly patient, God cared tenderly for their fearful, broken hearts. "You can trust me!" God told them. "I'll give you everything you need to live and flourish. Watch and see!" Just as a parent provides their baby with milk or tucks a blanket around a sleeping child, so God blanketed the land with good food the next morning.

As the people stepped out from their tents, they marveled at the white flakes that covered everything. This mysterious food seemingly dropped out of the sky. "What is it?" they asked one another as they giggled and nibbled and gathered. They worked together, gathering and sharing before the afternoon sun melted the flakes like magic.

"You can trust God with tomorrow's hunger," Moshe (Moses) told them, "so only gather enough for today." But God's people had been enslaved and were used to going hungry. Some of them did not trust God right away. They were scared and sad. Grabbing for God's gifts, they hoarded extra in their tents, but it just rotted and stank. There was only one day when the people were allowed to gather extra food, and it was for a very special reason. "Gather double on the sixth day," God instructed. "The seventh day is for Sabbath rest."

Rest? This was a new idea for God's people. For more than four hundred years, they had worked hard and miserable days. They were used to being tools in Pharaoh's power machine. They were used to doing, doing, doing. Making, making, making. And now God was asking them to just . . . be? *Don't you know that I love you not because of how many bricks you can make?* God seemed to be telling them. *I love you because I made you. Nothing can stop my love.*

Rest requires trust. Just as they had to trust God to feed their bellies, they also had to trust God to feed their aching hearts. To fill them up and tell them they were loved for who they were, not just what they could do. Morning by morning, they learned to trust God for the day's food. And week by week, they set aside a whole day just for resting. No more making and doing. On Sabbath, they played, sang songs, watched the stars, marveled and cried, and remembered and healed.

And slowly they released the ways of Egypt. Safe in the wilderness, reliant on God alone, they spent their days and weeks feeding and finding their trust. Those were the rhythms of remembering, the gifts of a good God.

WONDER MOMENT

WHAT IS IT? WHEN GOD'S PEOPLE SAW THE FLAKY substance on the ground, they called it *manna,* which means "What is it?"

Experts today have all kinds of theories about what manna was back then. Some say a miracle—bread rained down from heaven. God is certainly big enough for that!

Some say it was sap from nearby trees.

Some say it was beetle cocoons.

Some say it was secretions from insects that lived on the desert plants. That's right—bug juice! Bug juice that hardened into sugary droplets.

The writers of the Bible stories say that it was white and tasted sweet. What does that make you think of?

Cereal?

Coconut?

Marshmallows?

What *is* it?

We don't know! But what we do know is that on good days and on hard days, God will still be there when we wake up, making sure that we have enough.

THE MOUNTAIN
OF GOD

EXODUS 19–31; 36–40

Moshe is also called Moses. Tziporah is also called Zipporah.

P, UP, UP. GOD'S PEOPLE TIPPED THEIR HEADS BACK as far as they could, and still they couldn't see the top of Sinai, the mountain of God. They had crossed the wilderness to this holy mountain, and Moshe (Moses) was up there . . . somewhere.

They heard distant thrums and rumbles. *Was that thunder or . . . God?* Thunder or no thunder, when Moses came back down the mountain, he had a message from God.

Beloved, you saw my power against Pharaoh. You felt my flight of rescue from Egypt. Didn't I carry you, like a great mama bird, back to this nest to care for you? I've protected and provided for you. Have you come to trust me yet? Do you want to stay with me? I will guide you in my ways and show you how to live with peace and purpose.

If you are faithful to me, we can work together to heal the world.

God wanted to show the world what God is like.

They'll know I am different because you are different. They'll know my love through your love. They'll know my salvation through your safety. Through you, I can bless the whole world.

I promise to belong with you. Will you promise to belong with me?

And the people shouted their agreement: "Yes! Yes! We promise! We want to work together!" So God spoke to Moses for a long time from Sinai, shaking the mountain with a booming voice blazing like fire from above.

First, God gave him the Ten Commandments: words of wisdom to remind them how to love God and love people. They had lived for a long time in Pharaoh's power machine, and God was showing them how God was different and how they could be different too. In the same way Tziporah (Zipporah) had shown Moses a new way to use his staff, God was showing the people a new way to live together. The type of togetherness that creates life and flourishing, with God right in the middle of it.

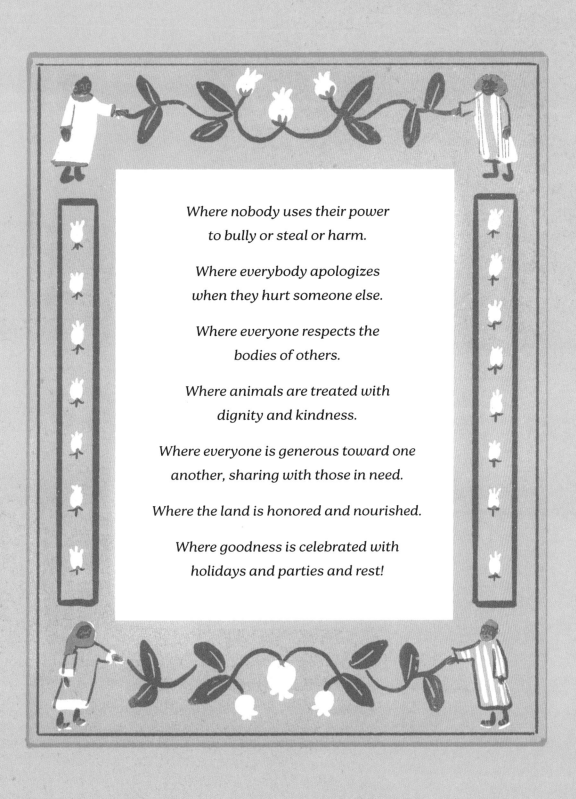

*Where nobody uses their power
to bully or steal or harm.*

*Where everybody apologizes
when they hurt someone else.*

*Where everyone respects the
bodies of others.*

*Where animals are treated with
dignity and kindness.*

*Where everyone is generous toward one
another, sharing with those in need.*

Where the land is honored and nourished.

*Where goodness is celebrated with
holidays and parties and rest!*

Doesn't that sound like a wonderful way to live? God's people certainly seemed to think so, because they shouted again, "Yes! Yes! We promise! We will do all these things!"

But as loud as they agreed, there were whispers of fear in their hearts. Yes, they had seen God's wonders, but in Egypt they had learned to be afraid of the person with power. They weren't sure they could trust God. So instead of meeting with God on the mountain, they sent Moses up alone. He was gone for a long time, and they grew worried.

The choices we make when we are lonely or scared are rarely our best ones. They often lead to sin as we hurt others and even ourselves. God's people had shouted their promises, but in no time at all, they broke them. Lonely and afraid, they fell back on all the ways they had learned to soothe themselves in Egypt. They made an idol, a small god they could see and touch. They gave the god presents to help their bad feelings go away. They tried to grasp for God's gifts—comfort, belonging, wisdom— without trusting God.

They did all the things they had just promised not to do!

But God stayed faithful, even when they were not. "I won't leave you, even when you leave me," God told Moses to say to the people. "I'll make a special place that reminds you of that." And then God gave Moses a blue-

print for the special place, called the tabernacle—a tent where they could go to meet with God. A place to take their complicated feelings about how they were living— their shame and their striving—and bring it to God. A beautiful place to reflect God's beauty and make them think of God's story.

Remember in the Garden of Eden when God made people? Creators and namers and caretakers? God reminded them of all these good names by letting them build God's tabernacle. It's as if God was showing them, *I made you to make things! Pharaoh abused that, but together we can heal. Use your hands for beauty and creativity. Work together, and don't forget to rest!*

The people brought fabric and jewelry and wood—the things they carried out of Egypt they now laid down to make a meeting place for God. All of them used their own unique skills, and soon the camp was alive with sounds of the project under way.

The *whish whoosh* of weavers making curtains. The *ping pang* of metalworkers hammering lampstands and curtain rings. The *tung tung* of the tent

frames and tables being built. And as they worked, God's words echoed in their hammering hands and hearts: *I won't leave you, even when you leave me. I promise to belong with you. Will you belong with me?*

They built and sewed and crafted, and finally the tabernacle was done and they all stepped back and grinned. It was splendid. Reds! Blues! Purples! Gold! Flower-shaped lampstands and intricate embroidery. A tent so beautiful and glorious that it shone against the backdrop of their encampment.

But it was about to become even more beautiful and glorious, because God came and filled it up with God's Spirit. God's Spirit hovered over the tent like a mother bird over her nest.

Or maybe it was like a lighthouse in the middle of a stormy ocean. Or like a parent sitting beside a bed while their child falls asleep. None of our words seem quite marvelous enough to describe what God's Spirit was doing. But the people's hearts swelled with comfort and joy seeing God in the middle of their camp.

And God stayed there, like that, through all their journeys together. God's Spirit remained, like a cloud during the day and like a glowing fire by night. Anytime the people felt worried or scared, they could look up, up, up and see God's beautiful reminder: *Nothing could make me stop loving you. I belong with you.*

FIVE FEARLESS SISTERS

NUMBERS 27; 36; JOSHUA 17

Mnasheh is also called Manasseh. Tzlafkhad is also called Zelophehad.
Makhlah is also called Mahlah. No'ah is also called Noah.
Khaglah is also called Hoglah. Milkah is also called Milcah.
Tirtzah is also called Tirzah. Moshe is also called Moses.

URING THOSE WANDERING-WILDERNESS DAYS, INSIDE the vast desert encampment of the People God Goes With, nestled among the tents of the Mnasheh (Manasseh) tribe, in the tent of Tzlafkhad (Zelophehad), there lived five fearless sisters: Makhlah (Mahlah), No'ah (Noah), Khaglah (Hoglah), Milkah

(Milcah), and Tirtzah (Tirzah). Girls so smart and kind that they moved with courage wherever they went. After all, do you know that courage means to tell the story of who you are, with your whole heart? Those girls knew who they were, and it made them brave.

And whenever they started to forget and feel afraid or lost, all they had to do was repeat their names:

> *Daughters of Zelophehad.*
> *Family of Manasseh.*
> *Camp of Israel,*
> *the People God Goes With.*

They were snug and secure at the center of so much belonging.

But one horrible day, Zelophehad died and the sisters found themselves afraid and confused. The rules in those days said that only a male could keep his father's things—including his name, his tent, his animals, his money, and, most important, his place in the Promised Land, where they were headed. So without a brother, the girls felt their layers of belonging start to slip away.

Daughters of . . . Nobody.

In the tent of . . . No One.

From the family of Nobodies . . . the People God Goes With?

I HAVE A PLAN.

It just didn't add up.

"What will happen to us?" worried Tirzah. She was the youngest and was quite used to being taken care of. "Will we have to leave our tent? Live with another family? Give up our special place in the Promised Land?" Milcah and Hoglah were filled with questions too. They had often daydreamed together about the Promised Land, wondering what their new home would look like, what types of food they would grow, how tall the trees would be. "This isn't right," said Noah. She was the boldest of the

sisters and always filled with good ideas. She huddled her sisters up in a tight circle, and together they made a plan.

The next morning, they walked arm in arm to the tent of meeting—the place where the priests gathered and God met with Moses. The sisters had talked late into the night. They knew who they were: They were the daughters of Zelophehad, from the tribe of Manasseh in the people of Israel. But most of all, they knew that they were loved and valued by a God who invites us to wrestle. They knew that even without boys in their family, God was still with them. And when you know who you are and whose you are, you know how to ask for what is right, even when it's scary.

Finally, it was their time to speak. Mahlah cleared her throat, took a deep breath, lifted up her chin, and explained what they had talked about all night: that their father had died but had no sons. That Mahlah, Noah, Hoglah, Milcah, and Tirzah loved God with their whole hearts and dreamed of their special place of belonging among the people of Israel. That they understood that the law said their inheritance was lost to them now.

"This is not right," said the five fearless sisters. They stood in front of Moses, Eleazar, and all the other Important People with Important Jobs and said, "Give us our land. We belong just as much as any sons would. We know who we are, we know whose we are, and we know it is right for us to belong."

The Important People with Important Jobs looked at one another. Girls as important as boys? This is a new idea. Let's see what God has to say about *that.* So Moses went to meet with God, and what do you think God said? "Of course!"

God said to Moses, "These five sisters are right. Give them their inheritance, just as they asked. And while you're at it, write this down and make it part of the law: Daughters have as much right to land as sons."

Moses came back with the news, and word spread from one tent to another: Mahlah, Noah, Hoglah, Milcah, and Tirzah had done it! Those five fearless sisters believed who God said they were more than they believed anyone else. And they changed the future for many girls to come.

REMEMBER TO REMEMBER

DEUTERONOMY 1–32

Moshe is also called Moses.

EMEMBER TO REMEMBER TO REMEMBER TO remember." Moshe (Moses) had been talking to God's people for a very long time. They would reach the Promised Land soon, and Moses was passing on instructions from God on how to live there.

It was a hot, windy day, and the people were bored and itchy. And it's hard to listen when you're bored and itchy. So after a while, all the important words Moses was saying sort of just sounded like that: "Remember to remember to remember." *Blah, blah, blah.*

Moses was a very old man now. He wasn't entering the Promised Land with them, so he filled his farewell speech with so much advice that if we told it to you now, you'd probably get very bored and very itchy. Here are the three important parts:

1. REMEMBER WHERE YOU CAME FROM. Moses reminded them of their stories and the stories of their ancestors, hoping they could see God's love for them woven throughout like a bold red thread creating patterns in a tapestry. A rescue here. A visit there. Oh, and don't forget that miracle!

2. REMEMBER WHO BELONGS IN THE MIDDLE. "Love God with every part of you. And remember to choose leaders who love God too!" Moses reminded them. "Leaders should let their love flow out to the people who need it most. Don't forget about them! Don't forget about the foreigners, the children without parents, and the widows. Nobody should be without belonging. Don't push them to the outside of the group; put them right in the middle, like they're covered in a hug."

3. REMEMBER WHERE YOU'RE GOING. Their time in the wilderness had been long, spanning generations. There were plenty of detours and missteps along the way. But God's people had always been heading toward the Promised Land. They had always been meant to be blessings to the world. God was doing a new thing in a new place.

"You've had so much special time in the wilderness, close to God and far from anything and anyone else," Moses said as he sent them forth into the new land. "Now it's time to go and choose God. Now it's time to go and bless everyone else."

You will feel fear.
When you feel fear, remember.

You will feel lost.
When you feel lost, remember.

You will feel shame.
When you feel shame, remember.

God's love stretches in both directions,
into all your yesterdays and all your tomorrows.
God is the same, and God will be with you
wherever you go.

Remember to remember to remember.

JUDGES

TIME PASSED, AND SO DID GENERATIONS. BABIES born in the Promised Land became parents and then grandparents. The stories of wonder and awe grew old as well, and eventually God's people forgot. They forgot about their suffering in Egypt and how God led them and fed them, dwelled among them, and called them by name.

They forgot that Moses told them, "Remember to remember to remember to remember to remember!"

They forgot the way God taught them to live: caring for the forgotten, welcoming others, making sure everyone had enough. They ignored God's names for them and turned to other gods, other pastimes—anything to help them feel safe, loved, belonging, and good.

God had warned them that while they listened to God, they would get to live in the land, but that if they didn't listen, there would be trouble. And there was lots of trouble! Those were dark and disastrous days, but God was still with them, where God belonged.

Time and again, God used ordinary people to rescue Israel from the messes they created. Ordinary people like A'tniel (also called Othniel), who was filled with God's Spirit. Ordinary people like Ehud, who fought with one hand. Ordinary people like Gid'on (also called Gideon), a farmer who spoke to angels. These people were called judges, and God used them to shine light in the dark, to bring God's people back to the path whenever they forgot.

A FIERY WOMAN

JUDGES 4-5

Dvorah is also called Deborah. Yavin is also called Jabin.
Ya'el is also called Jael.

HE PALM FRONDS SHIMMIED IN THE BREEZE, sounding like whispers to the people gathered below. And maybe they *were* whispering, because the woman sitting against the trunk seemed to hear words no one else could.

Dvorah (Deborah) was a friend of God. Every day, she would go sit under her palm tree, listen to God's voice, and help God's people with their problems. Her job as a prophet and judge required lots of wisdom. And just as a torch is lit from a source, so Deborah's wisdom came from God, burning steadily in her heart. And when she spoke God's words, full of justice and compassion, it was as though she breathed gentle fire. People came from all over the land to visit this fiery woman, desperate for a flame to light their way.

In those days, a king named Yavin (Jabin) had invaded the land and brutally oppressed God's people. As the darkness grew heavy and the people cried out once again for rescue, God spoke to Deborah with a message for Barak, a warrior whose name means lightning.

"God says it's time to gather your best soldiers and fight back against King Jabin," said Deborah. Barak looked for a long time at Deborah sitting under her palm, which stretched up to the heavens, showing the way with God's words as she always had. It was comforting to Barak to be with someone so familiar with God's voice and ways.

"I'll go if you go with me," said Barak finally. "But if you won't go, I won't either."

"Of course I'll go with you," assured Deborah. "But remember, God decides who will win, not you. In fact, the hero of this war will be a woman."

And so Barak and Deborah set out with the Israelite troops against the army of King Jabin. There was bravery and boldness, compassion and cowardice. In the end, Deborah was right: It was a woman, named Ya'el (Jael), who tricked the leader of Jabin's army and ended the battle.

After the clanking and shouting of battle died down, there was stillness and the rustling of palm fronds. Deborah closed her eyes and listened. The fight was over; God's people were free. *God is still with us,* she thought. *God is still speaking. But will anyone join me in listening?*

Looking out at the newly liberated people of God, Deborah opened her mouth and sang what she knew: a beautiful song about the God they had forgotten, the true names they had rejected. Barak joined in, and together the woman of torches and the man called lightning sang out:

> *May the enemies of God be silent*
> *And God's friends shine like Jael,*
> *Like the sun as it rises in its might.*

And God's friends became a flickering reminder in the darkness of forgetting. Justice shimmered across the land, lit from the Source of all light. And God's light shone in the darkness as there was peace for forty years.

15

WINGS OF POWER AND PROTECTION

RUTH 1-4

Na'ami is also called Naomi. Arpah is also called Orpah.

RUTH LOOKED AROUND AND FOUND no one to help. Behind her, just the worn and familiar road back to her home-land. Before her, the unknown road to Na'ami's (Naomi's) homeland. And beside her, Naomi and Arpah (Orpah). Three women, alone in the world.

Orpah kissed Naomi, hugging her tightly, and then turned and took the road behind. "Look, Ruth!" said Naomi. "Your sister-in-law is going back to her people and her gods. You should go back with her, as I have nothing to offer you!"

But Ruth was a woman of power and protection. Belonging burned bright in her, and she would not leave her mother-in-law. "Enough of that," Ruth said firmly. "Don't ask me to turn away from you. I belong with you, and you belong with me. Your people are my people, and your God is my God. I promise to stay with you, no matter what."

But Naomi just shook her head as they set off down the

road before them. When they arrived in Naomi's old village, Naomi's former neighbors and friends crowded around in shock.

"What a joke, to call me Naomi," Naomi said with a sharp laugh. "That name means delight, and as you can see, I have none. You should call me Mara, because God has made my life so bitter." In a dull voice, Naomi told them her sad story. How she left ten years ago with her husband and sons in search of food. How they settled in nearby Moab, where her sons married local women. How her husband had died and so had her sons. "When I left you, I was full. But God made me empty. No husband, no sons—in our world, that leaves me helpless. God has left me alone."

You're not alone. I'm right here, Ruth thought sadly as she stood beside Naomi and stared back at the curious crowd. They didn't like people from Moab, and it showed in the gawks and the whispers. Foreigner. Outsider. Helpless. Nobody.

Perhaps I should change my name as well, thought Ruth.

But the next morning, she woke with determination. She went to the fields outside town, in search of food, belonging, and blessing. She found them in the field of Boaz, a man of power and protection. Boaz still remembered God's ways. He remembered those in need by leaving the corners of his fields unharvested, available to the hungry and helpless. *I am hungry. But here is help, and I can be a helper,* Ruth thought, and she toiled all day, gathering grain at the corners of Boaz's field.

Boaz arrived at the fields, booming blessings to his workers and friends. Approaching Ruth, he spoke with kindness and welcome. Ruth looked around, surprised. *Is he talking to me?* She asked, "Why are you being so kind to me? You know I'm an outsider, right?" Boaz paused and then simply said, "I've heard about the kindness you've shown Naomi. Her people are now your people, and her God is your God."

And then, in the way that seemed so natural to him, Boaz boomed a blessing over Ruth as well, speaking true and beautiful words. "May you find blessing and comfort under God's wings." And Ruth smiled as she worked, Boaz's blessing echoing in her mind. She imagined God as a giant hen, keeping her safe and warm. *I belong with you, and you belong with me. Your God is my God.*

When Ruth arrived home that evening, her arms were full of more grain than she could carry, and her heart was full of promise. "Where did this come from?" Naomi was astonished, her eyes dancing with relief and delight and perhaps even hope. In a bright voice, Ruth told Naomi her glad story. How she found help in the corners of a nearby field. How the workers were respectful and the owner spoke kind words to her. "Boaz? Did you say Boaz?" Naomi interrupted, her grin blooming full on her face. "Boaz is a close relative of mine! We are two women, alone in the world, but he could help us belong again!"

Perhaps things are not as dark and disastrous as I'd assumed. Perhaps God has not forgotten us, Naomi thought over

the following weeks as Ruth returned to Boaz's field again and again. Ruth was always greeted with kindness and respect and returned with arms full of food for Naomi. And the kindness from Ruth and Boaz lit a fire in Naomi. It warmed and softened her, and she came up with a plan. It was dangerous, but women alone in the world must often battle dark and danger to get what they need.

So Ruth followed Naomi's plan. She crept through the night and startled Boaz awake. "Cover me with your wings," she challenged, tugging at his prayer cloak. "You're Naomi's close relative!" Ruth whispered. "I am helping her, but you can help us both. Marry me, and help us find safety and belonging." And as he stared at this bold woman, Boaz knew what she meant. He had prayed that God would help Ruth. But *he* could be the helper, the blessing.

And Boaz grinned. "I see you are a woman of power and protection," he said. "You've been kind to Naomi and helped her as God would." He knew he was being given a chance to do the same. He could follow God's ways and welcome others into belonging. "You're right. I will make it happen," he told Ruth as he sent her home in safety, arms loaded with food.

Ruth returned home as the sun was rising, and she poured Boaz's gifts into Naomi's lap. "Boaz did not want you to be empty. Neither do I." *You're not empty. You're not helpless. You're not alone.* And sometimes the true and beautiful words we speak to others help them believe the true and beautiful names God has for them. Naomi—once called Mara for her bitterness—began to delight again.

YOU'RE NOT ALONE!

And in the same way, as Boaz arranged the details for a wedding as quickly as possible, his names for Ruth helped others believe God's names for her. *She is Worthy of Love. She is Good. She Belongs.*

And so they built a home. Ruth, Naomi, and Boaz. A place of belonging where God's ways were cherished and kept. Their children and their children's children boomed blessing to others and spread their wings to comfort and shelter.

WONDER MOMENT

ON NIGHTS WHEN THE WINDS HOWL AND THE WORRIES coil around our bellies, the world can feel large and lonesome. Dark and dangerous. And sometimes it can be hard to understand why.

"Look for the helpers," the wise ones tell us. "There are always people of peace, power, and protection. They reflect God's light into dark places and help us to remember."

The story of Ruth sits in the Bible in the middle of so many stories of darkness. It's as if God is reminding us too, "Look for those helpers. Be the helpers."

In Naomi and Ruth's world, women without husbands or sons were in danger, no matter how brave or resourceful they were. So God told God's people to take special care of them and other groups lacking belonging. Boaz prayed for Ruth, and that was very good. But she reminded him (and us!) that God invites us to be helpers too. We get to join with God in blessing the whole world!

Think about your community. Who needs help reaching belonging? Who are the helpers? How can you be one?

16

SORROW TURNED TO SONG

1 SAMUEL 1-3

Khanah is also called Hannah. E'li is also called Eli.
Shmuel is also called Samuel.

 HANAH (HANNAH), MY HANNAH. WHY do you weep? Why won't you eat? Why is your heart sad? You have me—isn't that better than ten babies?

Hannah sat at the thanksgiving feast as the words of her husband, Elkanah, echoed in her head and made her chest tight. She had wanted a baby for so long that the yearning felt like a part of her, like it lived in her skin. But as time went by and her womb stayed empty, she grew silent and still, bottling up her feelings inside.

Why do you weep? Why won't you eat?

"I'm so sad and so angry," she finally blurted out to Peninnah.

The woman was Elkanah's other wife, so she just laughed and taunted Hannah. "So dramatic!"

"I'm so sad and so angry," Hannah told Elkanah.

He just scooped extra food onto her plate, waving away her tears. "You have me—isn't that better than ten babies? Isn't it?"

I'M SO SAD AND ANGRY.

But she couldn't eat. She couldn't ignore or put away her collection of sorrow and fury. It grew bigger and hotter in her chest until it felt like it was leaping up her throat to burn her tongue. Her hands clenched. Her jaw tightened. Her stomach churned.

Hannah ran to God's special meeting place, presenting her empty belly and empty arms before God and she wept. Big, shuddering gulps of sorrow. Hot, furious streams of tears.

"I'm so sad and so angry," she told God. It all spilled out of her: her bitterness, her pain, her sadness, and her fear. "I feel alone. I feel like I am too much. I feel like I am not enough."

She spoke true words to God and felt the ache in her chest release just a bit. "Oh, God-who-leads-the-angels, please remember me. If you hear my misery, would you give me a son? I promise I will give him back to you, every day of his life. I will teach him to listen to you and love you well."

As Hannah continued to pray silently, moving only her lips, E'li (Eli) the high priest interrupted, "Woman! Why are you acting so silly? Have you had too much wine? Stop making such a spectacle."

Hannah twirled to face him, her eyes and heart alight. "A spectacle? No, no. I am here with my big feelings—anger, sadness, bitterness, misery—all bottled up for many years. They are a real burden, but I won't bear them any longer. I am here to pour them out before God!"

"Ah yes," Eli replied gently. "God hears. May your dreams match God's own."

Hannah returned to the feast smiling and finally ate something. Her heart felt emptier yet fuller at the same time. It still ached with a mixture of sorrow and hope, but she no longer carried it alone. As they prayed and sang, she trusted God to hear and to hold her feelings.

Months went by, and Hannah's belly began to swell—she was going to have a baby! And when her son was born, Hannah delightedly named him Shmuel (Samuel), which means "asked from God."

God heard me when no one else did. I shared my whole heart, and God didn't try to shrink it down. God saw my sadness, my fear, my worry, and my deep yearning. I didn't hold back. And God heard. That is a true and beautiful thing.

As she nursed Samuel, she spoke true and beautiful things over him as well, feeding his body, mind, and heart. There are many stories we could tell about baby Samuel's long, lovely life, and they all started with Hannah's song.

"*God hears us,*" she sang. Samuel would grow up to hear God's voice as a very young boy.

"*People fail and forget, but God never gives up,*" Hannah sang. Samuel would grow up to see the great leaders of God's people fall into horrible, harmful ways. But he would search for God despite it all.

"*Someday God will raise up a new king, who will welcome God's ways,*" Hannah sang. Samuel would grow up to be a close friend of God. He would speak true and beautiful things to God's people. He would anoint and guide the first kings of Israel. And through that line of kings would come the truest king, the hope of humanity.

But for now there was just a mother's song, a thunderous wish fulfilled. And Samuel snuggled into her safety, surrounded by truth and trust.

THE MONARCHY

 OD'S PEOPLE GREW TIRED OF THEIR JUDGES. They looked at the nations around them, and what did they see? Empires led by kings or queens. Big and beautiful cities ruled by power and defended by armies. In comparison, their God-centered and God-ruled way of doing things felt . . . weak and backward. So they begged God for a king.

They had already forgotten *again* that God wanted them to be different. God didn't care about power and palaces and taking over the world; God cared about life and flourishing and blessing the world. "Do you remember what it's like to belong to a ruler?" God asked the people. "You won't be a family anymore. You'll become part of a power machine. You'll get hurt."

But they demanded a king, and they got one. And then another and another, in the way that kingdoms go.

The Promised Land became a kingdom, with power at the center instead of God. There were wise rulers and foolish rulers. War and peace. Flourishing and suffering. God's people would have many kings and queens, but the most famous of all was King David.

THE KING OF HEART

1 SAMUEL 16–17; 2 SAMUEL 6; 9; 11–12; PSALMS 13; 18; 94; 118

Mfivoshet is also called Mephibosheth. Mikhal is also called Michal.
Shmuel is also called Samuel.

AVID WHIRLED AND LEAPED, moving with surprising gracefulness for a warrior king. The whole city was singing, dancing, and praising God with everything they had, but nobody danced harder than David.

Clash smash went the cymbals! *Bweemp bweemp* went the trumpets! *Shicka shacka! Shicka shacka!* went the sistrums and the timbrels! And *shimmy-shimmy, shake-shake* went King David at the center of the party. No grand robes or stately nods. Just a king in common clothes, dancing like a commoner.

{ 126 }

Have you ever had such a big feeling that it seemed to skip past your brain and move your body all on its own? King David had lots of big feelings. They lived right under the surface of his skin, quick to flash and difficult to hide. And on that day, his body was thrumming with pure joy.

The ark was finally back! The beautiful gold box from God's tabernacle that reminded the people of God's presence had been lost for years. Now David had brought it back and planned to put it in the center of the city, right where it belonged. *Shimmy-shimmy, shake-shake.* This was good news indeed!

You see, of all the big feelings in David's heart, one of the biggest was a love for God. They were friends. God talked and David listened. And David talked to God too, pouring out his big feelings in prayers and passionate songs:

> *Don't forget me, God!*
> *You are like a song in my heart!*
> *With you I feel like I can climb walls!*
> *Help! I feel like I'm sinking and stuck!*

David shared his heart with God—every feeling, high or low. And there's something very bright and cozy about belonging with someone who has seen your whole heart.

Clash smash! Bweemp bweemp! Shicka shacka! David led the rollicking parade up the hill, toward the center of the city. It was a proud and delightful moment for him.

When God had chosen David as king so many years before, everyone was surprised. He was the smallest of seven brothers, still a little boy. But wise old Shmuel (Samuel) had looked deep into David's young face and said, "Man looks at the outside, but God looks at the heart." And the heart of David was not hard to see. It was large and loud, with all those big feelings coming out in bursts.

There were times when those big feelings tripped him. You know that God had many beautiful names for God's people: "You are Beloved. You Belong. You are Delightful."

But David's feelings were so big that sometimes he got overwhelmed. And instead of trusting in God's names for him, David would begin to believe *I am Sadness. I am Fear. I am Loneliness.* And at those times, David hurt and harmed. He grasped for God's gifts. He used other people's bodies to grab for what he wanted. He felt insecure and acted in a

greedy way. He felt angry and acted in a violent way. He felt powerless and acted in an abusive way. Because even kings chosen by God make terrible choices sometimes.

David's big feelings were true and important and powerful. When he trusted God's names for him, his feelings helped him unite God's people and remind them of God's ways: He felt angry and acted with courage, protecting his sheep from lions and protecting his people from giants. He felt compassion and acted with justice and kindness, sparing the life of Mfivoshet (Mephibosheth), the grandson of his enemy Saul. Mephibosheth was disabled, yet David invited him to the family table and made him an advisor. David felt sorrow and acted with humility. After his messes and missteps, he felt horror over the hurt and harm he caused. He admitted his mistakes, apologized, and trusted that he still belonged with God.

On days like today, when David trusted God's names for him, his big feelings became superpowers. They moved him to become a Blessing to Others. A Loyal Friend, a Fair Leader, a Generous Lawmaker, a King of Legends.

Shimmy-shimmy, shake-shake. The light reflected off David's crown as he danced and laughed. The celebrations continued as the ark was settled in its place at the center of

the city. He looked around at God's people, and his heart swelled with love. He wove through the crowds, handing out treats and kind words to the people he led and served. *Smash... bweemp... shicka... shacka... ssshhh.*

The music died off as the people returned home from a full day of celebrations. King David trudged back to his palace, all sweaty and disheveled and happy. His wife Mikhal (Michal) met him there, frowning and rolling her eyes. She had big feelings of her own—pain and worry—and they came through in her words.

"You embarrassed yourself today, dancing half-naked for the people like some sort of commoner!" But David laughed, loud and long. The ark coming back to the city felt so hopeful and important, like a beloved friend returning home. How could he explain how big his joy had grown? How could he *not* dance, knowing that God chose him to be king, God called him Beloved, and God's ark was back where it belonged?

"I was dancing for God!" David exclaimed. "If you think joy spilling over into dancing is embarrassing, well, I'll do even more embarrassing things than that! I'll dance with the commoners as we welcome God together!" And off he went, humming all the way.

18

WOMAN WISDOM

JOB 28; PROVERBS 1; 3; 4; 7; 8; 9; 14; MATTHEW 11; LUKE 7; 11

S TWILIGHT SETTLES ACROSS THE LAND, IN lamplit rooms and cozy alcoves, mothers and fathers tuck their children into bed. Stroking their hair and tickling their feet, they tell the old stories of Woman Wisdom.

Listen well, little one, for life is long and full of choices. Pay attention to your father's lesson: Don't forget your mother's teaching. There is a way these tender feet may walk well in God's good world. That way is lit by wisdom.

You might wonder, What is wisdom?

LISTEN WELL, LITTLE ONE.

TALK LESS AND LISTEN MORE.
MASTER YOUR ANGER.
DON'T LET FEAR GUIDE YOU.
TRUST GOD.
GET TO KNOW GOD'S WAYS.
SLOW DOWN AND BE STILL.
BE WILLING TO LEARN.
REMEMBER WHAT GOD HAS DONE.

Wisdom is woven throughout the universe. An invisible, glimmering thread. A guiding goodness. It helps us see right from wrong. It helps us treat others justly and generously. It's a glad voice calling us to live lives of love.

Sometimes wisdom seems like a path to walk on. It helps us avoid danger and leads to a good life. Sometimes wisdom is like voices that boom and whisper. Sometimes we feel it in our families' old stories as we remember what they did with their love and longings.

Sometimes we notice it in nature. The bustling of ants and squirrels saving up for cold weather. The direction of birds, the moaning of whales, and the skittering of bats. The knowingness of creatures and the steady sequence of seasons.

Wisdom is all around us, because God is here too!

The parents prattle on as the children cuddle close. The old stories describe wisdom as a person—a brilliant woman of welcome who shares her guidance with anyone who wants it. Woman Wisdom is old, they say. As old as the beginning.

When God was singing the Creation song, splitting seas and carving continents, Wisdom was there! She delighted in every new creation and creature, sometimes advising like a master crafter, sometimes cheering like a gleeful child. She rejoiced when God made people, agreeing with the good names God called us.

And she still calls those names. Shouting in the busy streets, bellowing through the gates of important castles, crying out from the steps of her house, Wisdom is always offering help, even to you. Even to me. Even today.

"Trust God," she reminds us.

"Get to know God's ways."

"Slow down and be still."

"Talk less and listen more."

"Master your anger."

"Don't let fear guide you."

"Be willing to learn."

"Remember what God has done."

Wisdom's words are pleasant, and all her paths are peace. She's like a tree full of fruit that gives life and happiness.

Eyelids grow heavy as the night grows darker and the mothers and fathers shush and soothe.

Yes, life is long and full of choices. Some days it feels like too many choices. But sleep well, love, for God has sent us a guide. Like Wisdom herself, God's Spirit is always speaking, delighting, advising, welcoming.

Wisdom promises to be found by anyone who needs her. Finding her feels like a big job, yes? But being in awe of that bigness is the first step to Wisdom. So may you awake with awe, my child, and listen when Wisdom speaks.

PROPHETS

HE KINGDOM OF ISRAEL SPLIT AND BECAME two kingdoms known as Israel and Judah. As their kings and queens rose and fell, God sent friends called prophetesses and prophets to light and lead the way. Like megaphones for God's wise words, these traveling truth-tellers carried messages to the people. Everyone from royals on their thrones to the merchants in town to the shepherds in the field heard from the traveling truth-tellers.

As the kingdoms stretched and grew, God's plan stayed the same: "Trust that you Belong, you are Beloved, and you are Delightful. Choose life and flourishing. Wrestle with me. Listen to Wisdom. Remember my ways to be a blessing to the world."

But it is difficult to choose peace over power. The kings and queens often didn't listen. They worshipped idols; they mistreated the poor; they didn't care for the people pushed outside belonging. They were greedy and violent and hateful, choosing a path of destruction instead of walking with God.

God was there and God was patient, sending prophetesses and prophets, one right after the other, to carry true names, messages, and reminders.

The traveling truth-tellers carried warnings and woes.

They also carried wisdom and hope.

Often people didn't trust that these messages were God's, spoken through the prophets and prophetesses. They ignored the traveling truth-tellers, mocked them, threatened them, and chased them away. And the louder the truth-tellers spoke, it seemed, the less the people heard, continuing to chase after idols and hurt one another.

But sometimes, yes, the messages were welcomed. Sometimes the people heard and turned back. Sometimes they loved God and loved people with fervor and faithfulness. And at those times, the land shimmered with shalom as they chose life and flourishing.

KHULDAH AND THE TINY KING

2 KINGS 22-25

Khuldah is also called Huldah. Yoshiyahu is also called Josiah.
Ydidyah is also called Jedidah.

NLY EIGHT YEARS OLD? MIGHT AS WELL CROWN a baby!"

"At least he has Queen Ydidyah (Jedidah) to guide him— she seems wise."

"A lot wiser than that worthless husband of hers!"

Khuldah (Huldah) the prophetess heard the whispers and chatter traded in the hallways and marketplaces. The king of Judah had been

killed and his crown placed on the tiny head of his son, Yoshiyahu (Josiah).

May Jedidah raise him to be a better man than his evil grandfather and father, Huldah thought, remembering all the horrors she witnessed in the years of their reign. As a friend of God, she had wept when she saw the blood that flooded the streets, the people hurt in the name of foreign gods, whose idols had been brought into God's temple. She had frowned as she walked the city streets, seeing the poor begging for help, women and children left without belonging, visitors cast aside. *Oh, people of God, this is not the way God taught us to live!*

But Huldah observed happily over the coming years that King Josiah appeared to be a very different kind of king indeed. Unlike his father and grandfather, Josiah chose God's path, not swerving to the right or to the left.

Josiah traveled the land and destroyed all the altars to false gods, where people and animals were misused and mistreated. Then he went into God's temple, the permanent place of belonging that King David had designed to replace the tabernacle tent. This special building, which was supposed to be for God, was now filled with idols and altars too.

Crash! Bang! Josiah tore them all down and then hired gifted artists and craftspeople to repair and restore God's temple.

And Huldah watched and smiled. *That's a good start, kid.*

Knock knock knock knock knock!

Huldah was startled one morning by a panicked sort of knocking at her door. She opened the door, and five men bumbled and tumbled over the threshold, all talking at once:

"We found an old scroll when we were cleaning the temple!"

"A scroll of Moses!"

"It has words in there from God!"

"King Josiah is very upset!"

"He knows we have not kept all God's ways!"

"What does God say?"

Huldah was quiet for long moments. She was a prophetess, and it was her job to share God's words: warnings and woes, comfort and courage. So she told them the sad truth that so many of the traveling truth-tellers had warned about: The kings before Josiah had made terrible, violent choices and led the entire kingdom on a path of destruction.

And despite King Josiah's changes, God's people were not living as they should. They weren't blessing the world as God had planned. In fact, they were acting worse than any of the nations around them. The hurt and the harm had piled up like trash dumped in a river. And even though

King Josiah had made rules that there was to be no more dumping, there was still trash in the river that everyone would suffer from for a long time.

It doesn't seem fair, does it?

You're right—it wasn't. Choices have consequences, and not just for us but also for the people around us and the people who come after us. That is why God had asked God's people from the very beginning to choose life and flourishing.

"Tell King Josiah that God sees him. God sees how his heart longs for God's ways and how he has tried to remind the people of God's good names for them. Consequences are coming, disastrous days are ahead, but for now Josiah will lead them in peace."

The men tumbled back out, carrying Huldah's message from God all the way back to the palace. And King Josiah took heart. As a good king should, he led by example. He gathered all the people in the city and read them the old scroll. He remembered the words of God and celebrated God's belonging with the people. He even threw a big party just like the one they had at Sinai and invited the people to renew their old promises.

"We promise to belong to you and be blessings to the whole world!"

"We promise to care for the forgotten among us!"

"We promise to rest on Sabbath and remember who we are and who we belong with!"

And they did! As long as Josiah lived, the people followed his leadership and kept their promises to God. And Huldah smiled. *That's a really good start, kid.*

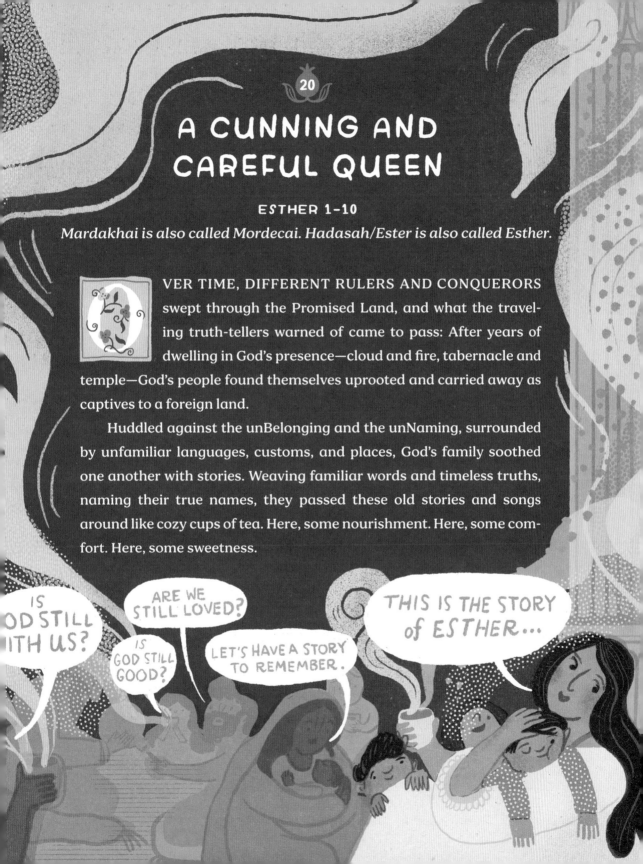

A CUNNING AND CAREFUL QUEEN

ESTHER 1–10

Mardakhai is also called Mordecai. Hadasah/Ester is also called Esther.

OVER TIME, DIFFERENT RULERS AND CONQUERORS swept through the Promised Land, and what the traveling truth-tellers warned of came to pass: After years of dwelling in God's presence—cloud and fire, tabernacle and temple—God's people found themselves uprooted and carried away as captives to a foreign land.

Huddled against the unBelonging and the unNaming, surrounded by unfamiliar languages, customs, and places, God's family soothed one another with stories. Weaving familiar words and timeless truths, naming their true names, they passed these old stories and songs around like cozy cups of tea. Here, some nourishment. Here, some comfort. Here, some sweetness.

IS GOD STILL WITH US?

ARE WE STILL LOVED?

IS GOD STILL GOOD?

LET'S HAVE A STORY TO REMEMBER.

THIS IS THE STORY of ESTHER...

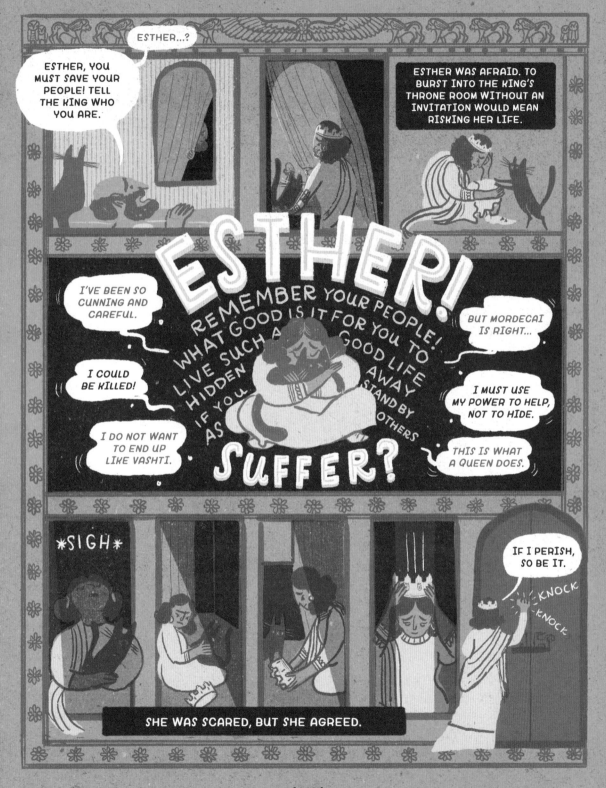

{152}

{ 153 }

I NAME MORDECAI MY SPECIAL ASSISTANT!

AND I HONOR MY QUEEN ESTHER FOR HER WISDOM AND BRAVERY!

TOGETHER MORDECAI AND ESTHER ASSISTED THE KING IN WRITING A NEW LAW THAT WOULD HELP GOD'S PEOPLE TO FIGHT BACK. ALL THROUGHOUT THE LAND, BULLIES WHO HAD HOPED TO HURT THEIR PEOPLE NOW FELT AFRAID.

I WAS CUNNING AND CAREFUL, AND NOW MY PEOPLE ARE SAFE.

AND SO, THANKS TO ESTHER AND MORDECAI, GOD'S PEOPLE SURVIVED.

And so God's people sipped and sighed, drawing comfort from Esther's courage, remembering their names, even as they lived in exile. Listening to Wisdom, searching for God, even when all seemed forgotten.

And to this day, once a year they put on costumes, break out their instruments and their cozy drinks and their familiar foods, and tell the story of cunning and careful Queen Esther as they celebrate a God who is there, even in disguise.

SEARCH for GOD.

MINDFUL MOMENT

MAKE YOURSELF A CUP OF SOMETHING HOT AND COZY. Sip and notice the way it warms your body from the inside out.

Wrap one hand around the mug and observe how it feels different from your other hand. Now wrap your warmed hand around your other hand and see how that feels. Put your face close to the mug. How does the steam feel on your face and up your nose?

As you enjoy your warm drink, think back over your day and search for God. Were there any moments when you felt alone? Were there any moments when you noticed God's goodness? What do you think tomorrow will hold?

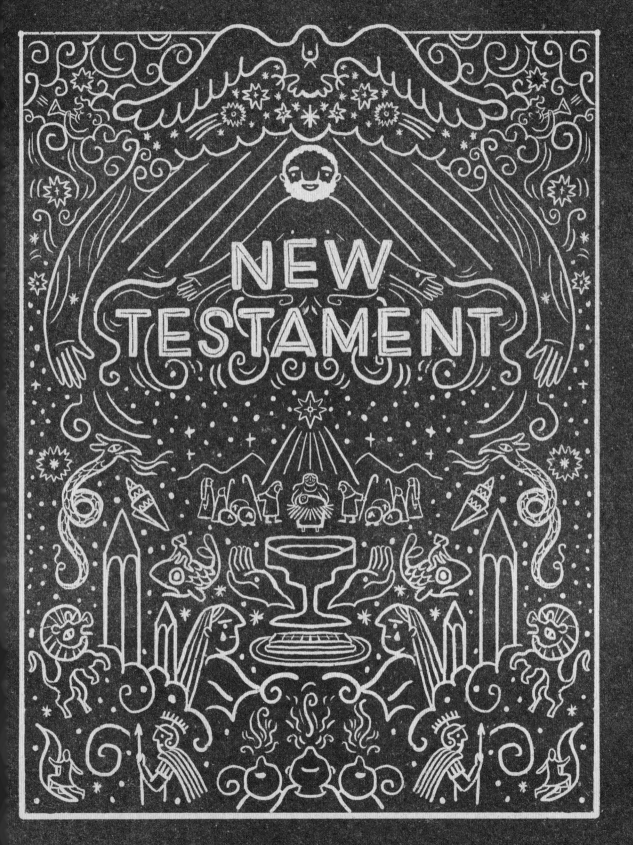

LINEAGE OF LOVE

"We are called Beloved, but we feel forgotten." "Things are not as they should be." "But someday God will become one of us and make all things new."

From Khavah (Eve) to Sarai (Sarah) to Miryam (Miriam) to Khanah (Hannah), to moms and dads we haven't even mentioned here, the name *Beloved* was passed down through God's people, tattered but steadfast. Whispered in the ears of nursing babies, murmured amid forehead kisses and trailing tears. In the grand stone turrets, in hushed desert tents, under the dome of stars, God's promises passed from family to family, generation to generation, timeless reminders of their true names:

"Be still, little one. You Belong with God."

"Take heart, dearest. You are Delightful to God."

"Sleep sweet, my child. You are Beloved of God."

Beloved, God's people breathed when they returned from captivity to their Promised Land, grieving and wondering how to recover. They rebuilt their cities, rebuilt the temple, and studied God's words and ways.

Beloved, they sang, even as new armies marched through the Promised Land and new power machines took hold.

Beloved, they insisted, even as the Roman power machine tried to control with swords.

Beloved, they clung to the truth, even as their own religious leaders tried to control with rules and shame.

God's names for them became shelters, stones in the mire, lights to burn back the crouching dark. They trusted that God would send a rescuer—a Messiah—because they were Beloved. *Beloved. Beloved. Beloved.* They repeated it day after day, year after year.

And then one day, an ordinary day, an ordinary girl gave birth to Love.

A MOMENTOUS MISSION

LUKE 1

Miryam is also called Mary. Yosef is also called Joseph.
Yeshua is also called Jesus.

IRYAM (MARY) WAS A COLLECTOR. NOT OF STONES or feathers or coins but of memories. Lovely moments were uncommon in a life like hers. A poor teenage girl engaged to a poor carpenter from a poor tiny village in the grip of the new Roman power machine. Life was not easy, but Mary seemed to know that there is always beauty for those who are looking.

So whenever life gave her an especially lovely moment, she held it gently. She examined it from every angle. Then she wrapped it up carefully and tucked it into the safest folds of her heart to savor later. She had all kinds of lovely moments, stored in her heart as if in a treasury. Such a heart makes a person kind and courageous. Such a heart keeps a person soft and wise, even when life is hard.

And Mary's life was about to become especially hard and especially lovely, all at the same time, because on that most ordinary day, an angel appeared to Mary. "Hello, dear friend of God!" the angel exclaimed. As you can imagine, Mary was startled—and a little confused. "Don't be afraid!" the angel said. Then the angel laughed, a pleasant sort of rumble.

"I'm here to announce a great adventure: You're going to have a baby!"

A baby. A baby. A baby.

The angel's words echoed in her ears, and all she could do was stare as the magnificent visitor continued to speak. "You will name your baby boy Yeshua: Jesus. He will guide and comfort God's family of belonging. He will rule like a king except that his kingdom will never end!"

Mary lifted her chin. This was an intriguing adventure indeed. Her heart sang out with courage and questions. "But how is this possible? I can't make a baby on my own!"

The angel went on to reveal a marvelous mystery: The same Spirit of God that danced and delighted to God's Creation song in the beginning, the same Spirit that turned emptiness into goodness, was going to create a life in Mary's womb. A miracle.

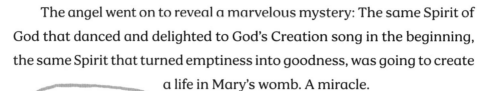

IF GOD SAYS I CAN DO THIS, I WILL.

Heaven was coming to earth. God was becoming a person. The angel laughed again, and the rumble of it seemed to wrap Mary like a hug. "Nothing is impossible with God!" he whooped. Mary was stunned. In a matter of moments, her entire life had changed. She held the moments gently, turning them over in her heart like crystals catching the light.

A baby that is God? God as a baby?

Will anyone believe me? What will my parents think?

What will my fiancé, Yosef (Joseph), say?

God is asking me to do this?

Why me?

Oh, the bittersweet ache of it all. But Mary, friend of God, had a heart full of trust and treasure. She felt it beating brave and full inside her chest. She took a deep breath. "I trust God," she finally said. "If God says I can do this, I will."

MINDFUL MOMENT

TRUST GROWS OVER TIME. THIS IS TRUE IN ANY relationship. One of the ways we learn to trust God is by noticing God in the little sneak-peek moments throughout the day. Mary was really good at this!

Close your eyes and think back on your day. What lovely moments did you tuck into your heart?

See if you can go on a treasure hunt this week. Anytime you notice a special moment—one that makes your heart glow—collect it! Like a leaf that's the perfect shade of orange. Or the ticket stub from a movie you saw with one of your parents. If it's something that happened in your head or heart, you could write it down or draw a picture.

You can collect your treasures in a special box and share them with your family at the end of the week.

THE KIDS WHO HEARD
THE GOOD NEWS

LUKE 2

Miryam is also called Mary. Yosef is also called Joseph.
Yeshua is also called Jesus.

NORES AND SNUFFLES FILLED THE COOL NIGHT AIR as a flock of sheep snuggled in the grass. In the distance, the city glowed and grumbled.

Across the field from the sheep, the shepherds chattered around their campfire. Shepherding was a job for the young, and most of them were the babies of their families. Gathered there, they looked like

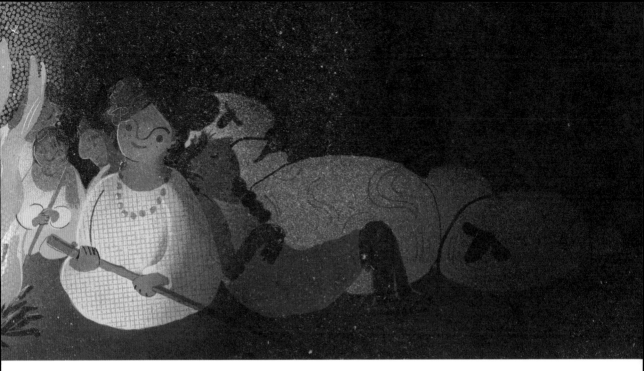

their own kind of flock. Some tall and lean, some short and round, each one of them strong in the legs and quick with a sling.

"Phew, you stink!" one shepherd said to her friend.

"We're shepherds!" he responded. "Stinking is the best part of the job!"

And they all giggled. Shepherding was dirty, smelly work, and most of the important people in Bethlehem wanted nothing to do with this flock of kids. And that's why they were all there, sleeping in the fields outside town with the grass as their mattress and the stars for a blanket.

Yawning and cozy, the shepherds began to settle in for the night, but a sudden flash of light startled them all. Like a star visiting earth, something—Someone—appeared next to the campfire, glowing brighter and warmer than its flames. The shepherds screamed and fell to the ground as the sheep looked on. This was not like any person they had ever seen before!

The Someone shimmered and shone, with a voice like a warm wind as it ruffled the grass around them.

"Don't be afraid! I have good news to share that will fill everyone's heart with delight: Tonight, in your little town, a baby has been born. He's the one you've been waiting for! The Messiah!"

The shepherd girls and boys peeked up from their hiding places to peer at the messenger. "It must be an angel!" whispered one. *Scooch, nudge, shuffle.* Slowly, they stood and inched closer, drawn to the dazzling warmth. The angel smiled and continued to speak in that voice that filled the fields. "This will be the sign for you: You'll find this special baby all wrapped up and sleeping in a feeding trough!"

And the shepherds almost giggled at the thought. *If this baby is so special, why would they put him in the place where animals would snort and drool and gobble their food?* But the almost-giggles faded away into wonder as the sky above burst into riotous color and harmony. Like a thousand suns rising—Gold! Lavender! Orange! Pink! Crimson!—angels crowded to the horizon.

Hundreds, thousands, mil-
lions, gazillions, all singing with gleeful celebration.

"Praise! Praise! Praise! Heaven meets earth! May our
celebration and delight rise above the stars, and may God's peace be
with the people!"

Oh, what a celebration it was. It would have squeezed and
stretched your heart if you'd been there. Like the most beautiful sight you'd ever seen and the most wonderful
song you'd ever heard, all at the same time. The

sheep, the angels, and the shepherds danced and cried and stared and sang. And when the final note faded away on the last ribbon of light, the shepherds all spoke at once.

"Was that real?"

"Was it a dream?"

"The Messiah is here?"

"Why did they tell *us*? Nobody ever tells us anything!"

And they cried because their eyes had seen something of heaven. And they grinned with that shy, special mix of disbelief and pride. And feeling important for once in their little lives, they chased one another, tumble-bumble, back toward town to see for themselves what God had announced.

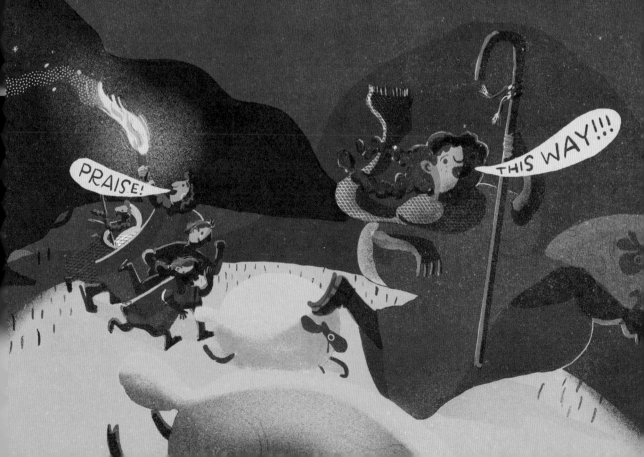

Imagine them, a group of stinky kids, running wild through the streets, peeking in windows and knocking on doors, being shooed and shouted at until—"Look, look! Over here! Wait for me!"—they found him. His parents' eyes shimmered and danced as the kids clamored to tell their story. Miryam (Mary) and Yosef (Joseph) had marvelous angel stories of their own to share. There were many hugs and happy tears and then a deep, warm, holy silence as they all stared into the feeding trough.

Because there lay Yeshua (Jesus), the rescuer the angels sang about.

Did the shepherds know the whole story of who they were looking at? Do we ever really know the whole story of who we are looking at? Maybe they knew, and maybe they didn't. Maybe, like us, they had peeks and nudges of God's Spirit and God's plan as they ran back into the streets, shouting the good news and singing everything in their happy hearts.

But God knew. God had always known, from the very beginning: "I belong with you, and you belong with me. You're my beloved."

In a garden, in a family, in a tabernacle, in a kingdom, and now in a person. Heaven and earth, bound up in a baby. The hope of the whole world.

BELOVED, BELONGING, AND DELIGHTFUL

MATTHEW 3; MARK 1; LUKE 3; JOHN 1

Yokhanan is also called John. Yeshua is also called Jesus.

UNLIGHT COMBED THROUGH DATE PALMS AND olive branches, striping the lazy waters of the Jordan River. Below the surface, the catfish swam, dipping and darting past the ankles of the man above. Yokhanan (John) was a familiar shadow to them. He was a friend of God and a relative of Jesus. He lived in the wilderness, that place of quiet closeness, and spoke true words to God's people. His voice echoed above the water, calling—always calling—for God's people to get ready.

"Something new is happening!" he called. "A rescuer is coming! Come, wash off those untrue names you've believed and trust God's good names for you. Repent! Turn from your sins and return to God, where you belong."

And many people did. They came and dunked under the water and put their hope in God. John reminded them that trusting God's names should change their actions too. "Be a blessing! If you have two cloaks, give one to someone with none. Do the same with your food!" "Don't use your power to harm! Don't cheat or steal!"

One day, a man stepped into the water to be baptized. John gasped—he knew this man. It was the baby the angels and shepherds had celebrated, all grown-up. The Great Rescuer. It was Yeshua (Jesus). *But what is Jesus doing here?* John wondered. "I should be coming to *you* for cleansing!" John sputtered. "Why would you come to *me*?" But Jesus assured John that it was all part of God's dream of belonging. So John trusted Jesus, and into the water Jesus went.

Dunking under for a moment, Jesus was gone, beneath the water with the catfish and quiet. Along the riverbanks, the people watched and waited. But Jesus burst to the surface again, and suddenly it was as though the world around him split open. It was as if the date palms and olive branches and riverbank peeled back to show a glimpse of heaven: God's world. Like a grin breaking open with joy, like a door creaking to reveal a room full of wonders. Light and love poured out.

God's Spirit emerged and, like a bright and beautiful dove, shimmered and settled upon Jesus, seeming to light him from the inside. As the crowd looked on with gaping mouths, they heard a noise that filled the horizon, calmed the waters, and danced among their cells and sinews. It was warm and familiar like all their very best stories and memories. It was the voice of God.

"This!" the voice sang out. "This is my beloved Son, who delights me." The voice of God rumbled across the ripples and eddies, beyond the river, echoing through the canyons.

It was a special moment. One that John would play over in his mind for the rest of his life. He didn't know the full story of God's dream, but he was right: Something new was happening. God's world—God's kingdom—was bumping up against the human world, spilling over. That peeled-back glimpse into God's world never quite closed again, and the Spirit stayed aglow in Jesus. It shimmered and settled and echoed through God's words.

"This child Belongs. This child is Beloved. This child is a Delight."

MINDFUL MOMENT

HEAVEN AND EARTH. SPIRIT AND FLESH. INVISIBLE AND visible. It's all very big and confusing sometimes, isn't it? There's so much to learn and wrestle with.

It is comforting to know that the same warm voice that spoke about Jesus speaks about us too. The same shimmering Spirit fills our hearts and horizons as well. The same words echo for me and for you. Put a hand over your heart and speak God's names for you: "I Belong. I'm Beloved. I'm a Delight."

JESUS'S DIVERSE DISCIPLES

MATTHEW 4; MARK 1; LUKE 5; 8

Shimon is also called Simon. Petros is also called Peter. Andreas is also called Andrew. Yaakov is also called James. Yokhanan is also called John. Matityahu is also called Matthew. Miryam the Migdal is also called Mary Magdalene. Thaddios is also called Thaddaeus. Philippos is also called Philip. Shoshana is also called Susanna. Ntanel is also called Nathaniel. Yokhana is also called Joanna. Yehudah is also called Judas. Shlomit is also called Salome.

WHAT'S A GROUP OF FISH CALLED? THAT'S RIGHT— a school. A school of fish live together, travel in the same direction, and care for one another.

Jesus had a school too. A group who lived with him and traveled with him from place to place and took care of one another. But maybe more like the schools you are used to, Jesus's school wasn't full of fish but instead was full of students. Women and men who were excited to learn from him who were called "disciples."

The first students who joined Jesus's school were—you guessed it!—fishermen. Jesus met Shimon (Simon) and his brother, Andreas (Andrew), fishing with their friends Yaakov (James) and Yokhanan (John), who were also brothers. Jesus told them, "Follow me! You have always used your nets for fish, but now your job and your joy will be to fish for people. You will find people, pull them close, and welcome them into my school."

So these fishermen left their boats behind and joined Jesus as he fished for people in many places where others wouldn't look. He held on to people whom others might throw back. He caught people who had been given names like Broken, Bad, Sick, and Selfish and renamed them. He pulled them into belonging like a fisherman gathering a net and said, "You're in *my* school now. Live with me; travel with

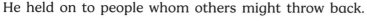

me; take care of one another. You don't need those old names."

"Shimon (Simon), your doubts are wild and wobbly, but I will call you Petros: The Rock."

"Matityahu (Matthew), you are not a Thief or a Cheat. Stop trying to fill your heart with money. Fill it with my love instead."

"Miryam the Migdal (Mary Magdalene), you're not Bad. You're not Sick. You're not Crazy. You're a migdal—a tower of truth! You're Loved. Come and belong with me."

Jesus's school traveled all over the land, fishing for people and holding them tight as Jesus called their names. Here's what they would sound like in English: "Thaddaeus! Philip! Susanna! Nathaniel! Jacob! Joanna! Judas! Salome!"

"These are wonderful names. I'm delighted by them and by you too. Come, follow me! Somehow each one of you is my favorite. You are so delightful to me."

And so Jesus's school grew and grew. And all kinds of different men and women were gathered up to belong, and they tossed away their old names. They stopped thinking they were made to be Smart or Lazy or Forgotten or Rich or Poor or Best or Least, because as they listened to Jesus teach and watched him live, something special happened. The more they heard about the kingdom of God, the more they wanted to live there, and the closer they wanted to swim to this man who already did. So they swam, a school of students, beautiful in all their differences and held close by the same goal: to believe in the names that Jesus called them and learn more about the kingdom he promised.

OUTSIDE-IN KINGDOM

MATTHEW 4-7

Yeshua is also called Jesus.

 ESHUA (JESUS) BECAME QUITE FAMOUS. NOT IN the worldwide way you may think of but in the way of small towns and irrepressible goodness. The way the best bakery in the valley becomes famous. The way the most beautiful sunrise view in the foothills becomes famous. People could not help but bubble over with the good news of what Jesus was doing.

At the wells, in the marketplace, through the vineyards, and under the stars, stories and whispers flew.

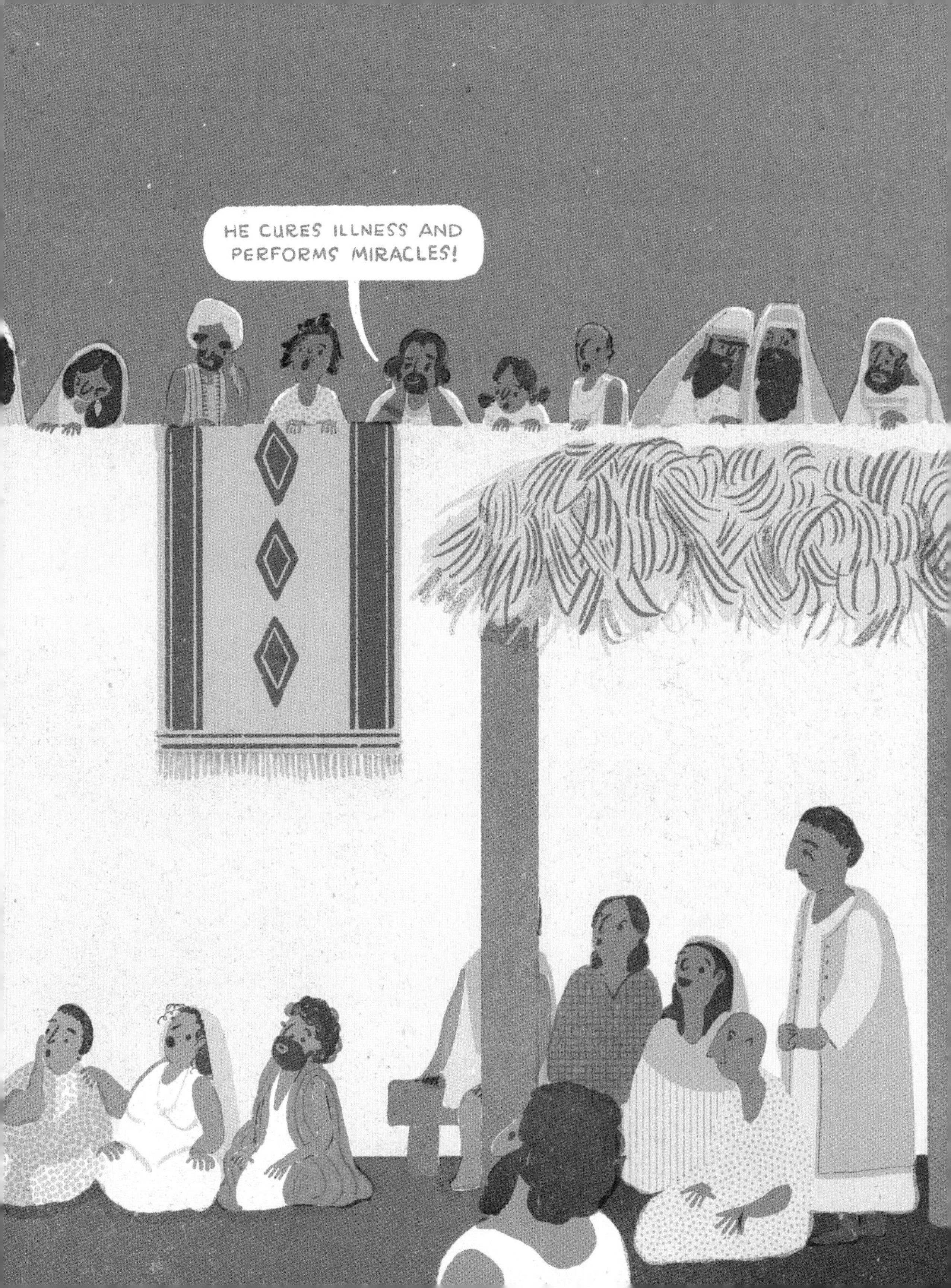
HE CURES ILLNESS AND PERFORMS MIRACLES!

And people began to flock to Jesus, like birds riding a warm wind. They brought him their sick friends to be healed. They waited to hear his teaching. They repented, returning to God and believing in their true names. Crowds covered the hillsides around where he stayed, made up of all kinds of different people. The sick, the scandalous, the poor, the pagan, the pious. People who would never, ever be seen together found themselves drawn to the same place for the same reason: Jesus.

On one particular day, the disciples were looking at the crowd, and Jesus was looking at the disciples. He saw their eyes jumping from person to person, naming them in their minds.

Nobodies. Mess-ups. Heathens. Failures. Rule-breakers. Outsiders. Jesus sighed.

We all know that it's hard to remember or believe who God says you are when other people are always calling you something different. This is why words and names are so important. Some of the stickiest names are the ones that convince us we don't belong with God. Names that really just mean Outsider. But Jesus knew that in God's dream, nobody is treated as an outsider.

God had always been telling God's people to trust God's names for them first. To invite others in. To care for the forgotten and give them new names like Belonging, Beloved, and Delightful. God made people to be like little mirrors. To reflect what God is like and to act like God in the world. And now Jesus would remind them about the lives for which they were made.

God's kingdom was spilling in, but it was going to look so much different than even Jesus's closest friends expected. So Jesus smiled and spoke gently to these friends, showing them how things were going to be.

"See these people? Their spirits are begging," he said, gesturing to the ragtag crowd. "And God is for them."

"God is for the sad, the gentle, and the searching. They see God's kingdom in new ways." Jesus's friends looked out across the hills, dotted with people eager for a taste of heaven on earth. People they were warned about. People they avoided. People they pitied.

Was Jesus really saying that there was goodness there? That God's blessing was on . . . *those people*? Jesus went on. "God is for the merciful, the honest, the peacemakers. Yes, *they* are here in this crowd too! They give us glimpses of God's kingdom—the kingdom of heaven."

Jesus knew this wouldn't be an easy lesson. Habits are hard to break, and God's people had many ideas about belonging, about who was in and who was out. Jesus's new way of thinking would divide people and create arguments.

"God is for you when others insult and reject you for acting like me. But you're supposed to light up the world," Jesus reminded them. "The way you act should show others God's love for them!" The disciples listened closely as Jesus continued to paint a beautiful and startling picture of what God's dream for God's people looked like. Some of it was familiar, and some of it felt brand-new. "Remember the mountain of God? When Moses told you how to love God and one another well? Watch me! I'll show you how to do that!"

Jesus spoke for a long time, with lesson after lesson. New ways to live. A new type of kingdom. *But when? When? When?* the people listening wondered. This hard and holy way of living that Jesus described sounded beautiful, true, and good. They wanted to live like that. But as they looked at the world around them—war and suffering and sickness and tears—it seemed unlikely, impossible!

Will it be an instant fix? How will things change? Is Jesus going to destroy the Roman power machine?

"No," Jesus told them in his mysterious way. "This is not like the violent clashes and conquests throughout history. God's kingdom is here . . . but also not here."

Here but not here? The disciples murmured and scratched their heads. *This is confusing.*

So Jesus wove together some word pictures, hoping to help them understand. "God's kingdom is spilling in bit by bit." He tried to show them. "It is already here, and

it has almost arrived. A kingdom of Already and Almost. It's like a tiny mustard seed that is planted and will grow to cover the hillsides. It's like the bit of yeast in a batch of dough that changes the way the dough looks and expands. It's like a net thrown into the water that catches fish of every kind. Things have changed and will continue to change. You're getting peeks and glimpses of what will someday be everywhere."

Jesus traveled from town to town with his friends. And everywhere he went, it was a show-and-tell about God's kingdom—what it was like, how they could live there. And to the people living in the small towns and villages, suffering under the Roman power machine, Jesus's message felt like the best hope they had experienced in a long time. Like a waft of warm bread first thing in the morning, like the first glimmer of sunrise over the foothills, it felt like goodness was peeking in at last. And they couldn't help but share.

WONDER MOMENT

WHAT IS THE KINGDOM OF GOD? WELL, IT'S NOT A place you can point to on a map. It's more like an idea. A way to live. A dream, really. It's God's dream come true. Imagine what a kingdom would be like if God were in charge. What would that look like? Feel like? Sound like?

Things would match God's dream: people belonging with God, caring for the earth, and blessing one another. Things that don't match what God is like? They aren't there! Things like suffering, cruelty, unfairness, even death.

Sometimes we simply call this heaven. Sometimes we call it the kingdom of heaven. Sometimes we call it the kingdom of God. And since most of us don't have kings or queens anymore, some people like to call it the kin-dom of God, because *kin* means family. And isn't that a beautiful thought?

Jesus came with good news: That kin-dom is happening now. That kingdom is happening now. That dream is happening now. The same way Jesus was God in a body, our world is now God's dream coming true.

What are your favorite names for God? What do they tell you about God's kingdom (or kin-dom!), a place or family that matches what God is like?

SIDE BY SIDE

MATTHEW 9; MARK 5; LUKE 8

Yeshua is also called Jesus.

HINGS ARE ALWAYS HAPPENING SIDE BY SIDE IN THE mix of heaven and earth. Life and tragedy and disbelief and joy. In one city, over twelve years, two daughters lived side by side. Strangers and neighbors, separated by circumstance.

One grew from a child into a woman, and pain found her in ripples, then waves. Her body bled and burned, sick in a way that baffled doctor after doctor. She spent every penny searching for a cure, but there was no cure, only mystery.

Believe it or not, some people don't like mysteries. Some people find mysteries to be very uncomfortable. Some people, especially those who like to be in charge, don't quite know what to do with mysteries. Because of their rules, because of her mysterious blood, they named her Unclean and put her out. Outside of her family, outside of the city, outside of worship, outside of belonging. And there she stayed and suffered.

Sweet and spicy, brave and brilliant, two daughters lived side by side. The other grew from a baby into a girl. She was her parents' only child, and she lived in sunshine and belonging. Her house was grand, her father was important, and her body was healthy until—so suddenly—it wasn't.

Tripping and gasping, her father ran through the city at a pace undignified for an important religious man. The crowd stepped aside when they saw him. "Yeshua! Yeshua!" ("Jesus! Jesus!") he cried, falling at Jesus's feet. "Please come quickly! My daughter—my light and my love—she's dying! Please, come and heal her!" Off they went, as quickly as they could through the crowd that squeezed and pressed. Strangers and neighbors, rich and poor, sunshine and suffering.

Outside the crowd, outside the city, the girl who was now a woman hesitated, watching Jesus. For twelve long years at the edge of belonging, she had suffered and studied. Full of pain, full of prayer. *He's right there. The mysterious Messiah. Heaven come to earth.*

She remembered the old promises, read from ancient scrolls. How they said a Messiah would come to rescue God's people and bring healing

in his wings. How they said all the people would leap for joy. With this hope in her heart, she snuck inside, thinking, *I just need to touch the wings of his cloak.* Into the city, into the crowd, pushing and squeezing and ducking and bumping, until—there!

Things are always happening side by side in the mix of heaven and earth. Hurry and hope and power and prayer. Jesus felt some of his power flow out, even as her flow of blood stopped. Her pain and her sickness, gone in a moment.

He turned, and as their eyes met, she couldn't decide whether to laugh or cry. Should she fall at his feet and cover him with thanks? Should she run and frolic like a happy little calf? Oh, the ache of a miracle.

Jesus knew. "My daughter—light and love—take courage." He smiled. "You trusted me! You're saved! Go in peace, free from torment." She hurried away with her good news, even as a messenger approached with bad news.

Two daughters lived side by side, strangers separated by circumstance. One felt life fill her weary body as tears of joy filled her eyes. The other felt life leave her body as a wail went up from the grand house.

"Your daughter has died. Don't trouble Jesus any longer. Nothing can be done." The messenger delivered his bad news. The crowd looked to the important man, who looked to Jesus. "Take courage," Jesus said. It seemed as if he said that often.

"Trust me." And what could the important man do but obey? Off to the grand house they went, greeted by wails and weeping. "Stop that," Jesus said. "Why the commotion? She's only sleeping." The wails turned

to bitter laughter. *Now, wouldn't that be something?*

Things are always happening side by side in the mix of heaven and earth. Cries and courage. Rest and resurrection.

Jesus took the girl's small, cold hand in his warm and weathered one. Death was a mystery to most. But mysteries did not make Jesus uncomfortable. He was there to show people what God's kingdom is like. The kingdom of Already and Almost, where death will be defeated.

So he brought her back in. *"Talitha koum!"* he said to the girl, warming her hand and her heart. *Little girl, get up!*

And what could she do but obey? Up she went, alive again, walking around like a little calf off to pasture. Wibbly-wobbly joy. Her parents were astonished. Should they laugh or cry? They did both, all at once, twirling their girl in a giggling, snuffling hug.

Two daughters lived side by side, and they savored the gift of growing old and grand. They moved through their days and their city with the thoughtful twinkle of those who have tasted heaven. One would say, "He ended my suffering and brought me back to belonging." The other would laugh. "He restarted my body and brought me back to life."

Oh, the ache of a miracle.

27

JESUS AND THE PARTY PEOPLE

MATTHEW 11; 23; LUKE 7; 11; 14

Yeshua is also called Jesus.

HAVE YOU EVER HAD THAT FEELING? THE feeling after a cozy meal, where you sit back and stretch your full belly, listen to your loved ones chatting and laughing under the twinkling lights, and everything just feels deeply *right*? Almost like a gentle lion reached out and put a warm, heavy paw on your chest? *Be here. Be still. Enjoy.*

There is something very special about sharing a meal. Something of heaven. Yeshua (Jesus) knew this better than anyone. As he traveled from village to village, he could often be found at the table, laughing, singing, sipping, and munching.

In fact, Jesus spent so much time at the table that some people were starting to whisper about him. "He drinks too much wine! He stuffs himself with

food! He goes to parties with the sinners and the outsiders!"

This was because the parties Jesus attended weren't in grand palaces or in the homes of the important and fancy people. He was feasting on the outskirts. In the run-down neighborhoods. At the houses of the forbidden and forgotten. With the people everyone else avoided, overlooked, or pushed outside of belonging.

Jesus's choices and actions told the same story his words did: *God's kingdom is already spilling in, and there are no outsiders here. God's kingdom is upside down and inside out. God's kingdom is a place of belonging.*

One day Jesus was invited to a very different type of feast at a very different type of house.

The house was full of scholars, religious leaders, and Very Important People. They talked in low voices about official things like rules and regulations and scriptures and obedience. Jesus then entered, messy and magnificent. They all began to do a special washing ritual before the meal, but Jesus did not join in.

"What good is it to wash the outside of a cup if the inside remains filthy? You are all so concerned with a spotless reputation, making sure you 'act' clean. But God sees your heart, full of greed and violence. But if you clean the inside of the cup, won't the outside become clean as well?" And as Jesus continued to speak, the Important People probably wished they had left him to party with the commoners, because he began to say things that left them shocked, uncomfortable, and just plain angry.

"You're so focused on rules that you've forgotten how to be a blessing! The guidelines God gave to Moses were meant to lift up the oppressed, but instead you crush them beneath a heavy burden—one you can't even lift yourself!"

The teachers and scholars shifted in their seats. *Who does he think he is? Is he questioning our traditions? Who would we be without our rules?* They were not used to being spoken to this way, thank you very much.

Jesus continued, "You love being the Important Ones. You get the best seats, and everyone in the marketplace knows your names! But the kingdom of God is upside down and inside out! That stuff doesn't matter!" Then, as he sometimes did, Jesus tried to teach them with a story, because sometimes our most important ideas can't be crammed into our specific words. They're too big and wiggly and special, so we have to say, "It's like . . ."

"God's kingdom is like a grand feast," Jesus began as the cups clinked and the candlelight danced. "Except when the food was prepared and the drinks were poured and the table set, the people who were invited did not show up! So the host told their servant, 'Go into the streets and alleys! Go to the run-down neighborhoods. Go to the houses of the forbidden and forgotten. Invite people who are poor. Invite people who are disabled. Invite people who are blind. Invite everyone and anyone who has been avoided, overlooked, or pushed outside of belonging.'

"'It's been done!' reported the worker. 'They have all joined your feast, but there is still room at the table!'

"'Then go,' urged the host. 'Shout from the highways and the walls. Urge the people to come and fill up my house!'"

Jesus looked around at all the important and fancy people at the table. People who had spent their lives memorizing Scripture and studying the rules. Oh, how he loved them. He saw how their worried hearts longed for God's kingdom. He saw how they were grasping for it in the best way they knew how. They were so close to the kingdom feast yet so far outside.

Jesus stood up to leave and the Important People became aggressive and mean. They hurled trick questions at him and schemed against him. But Jesus had work to do, and as the door swung shut behind him, they were left to their own private party, which had lost a bit of its sparkle.

CRASH BOOM

28
WALKING ON WATER

MATTHEW 14

Petros is also called Peter. Yeshua is also called Jesus.

RASH! BOOM! A FIERCE storm churned across the Sea of Galilee, and waves pummeled the small boat like giant fists.

Petros (Peter) had always felt at home on the wild and impetuous sea, perhaps because he was a bit wild and impetuous himself. Always blurting and bristling, Peter was a coil of constant energy waiting to be released. That had

BOOM CRASH

been helpful to him as a fisherman, but since following Yeshua (Jesus), he wondered if there was a place for his wildness with this peaceful teacher.

Peter squinted through the dark and downpour, as if he could see back to shore. Back to where he and the other disciples had sailed away from Jesus.

Jesus, who always showed him the way. Jesus, who always seemed to believe in him. Jesus, who gave him the name Peter, which means "rock."

Rocks stand firm, Peter thought as the wind tugged at him. *They also sink,* teased the doubts in his mind.

BOOM!
CRASH!
SPLASH!

TAKE COURAGE!

It was too dark to see his friends and too loud to hear their cries, but Peter could feel their worry. Could their little boat survive this raging storm? Then, through the sheets of rain and teetering waves, they saw a . . . something. *Too big to be a fish. Too solid to be a wave. Is it . . . a person? It can't be!* "A ghost!" They screamed and scrambled. They sobbed and shrieked. But then . . .

"Take courage," came Jesus's voice over the storming seas and the disciples' fearful cries. Jesus was walking to them across the sea. God in person, passing over the good creation.

"It's me! No need to fear,"

Jesus called. And though they were chilled to their chattering bones, his voice warmed them from within.

As often happened, Peter's words escaped his mouth before he could think. "Jesus, if it's *really* you, tell me to meet you on the water," Peter bellowed. *If you are who you say you are, ask me to come with you. If I am who you say I am, I should be able to.*

"Come along, then!" called Jesus.

The storm carried on around them. But Peter had a wild heart, and it loved Jesus fiercely. He felt it knocking on his ribs as he scooted down the side of the boat toward the raging sea.

Baboom. Worry.

Baboom. Excitement.

Baboom. Now worry again.

And then—*how?*—he was walking! He was doing what his teacher did. And with every impossible step, his thoughts surged.

He changed my name. He calls me Peter—the rock. My heart is wild, but he calls me solid. I belong with him. He belongs with me. I am beloved. Before Peter knew it, his feet had carried him across open sea, closer to Jesus.

But the thunder clapped and the wind roared and Peter's wild heart shook as the fear returned. *What if I'm not who he says I am? What if I don't belong?* His toes! His ankles! His legs! His knees! Ice-cold water gobbled them up as Peter began to sink.

"Jesus!" he shrieked. "Rescue me!" But Jesus knew. Jesus was near. He grabbed Peter and said gently, "Oh, Peter, with your tiny trust, why did you waver?"

Together, they returned and climbed back into the boat—Peter shaken, and Jesus calm. The calm was catching: At once the wind hushed up and the storm slunk away. As they watched the wilds of creation grow tame around Jesus, everyone on the boat fell to the ground.

"You really are God's Son!" they cried. And Peter looked on in amazement. *You are who you say you are. I am who you say I am.*

29

BE KIND TO ME

MARK 10

Bar-Timai is also called Bartimaeus. Yeshua is also called Jesus.

AR-TIMAI (BARTIMAEUS) CRACKED HIS KNUCKLES as he listened. He was very good at listening. A wind, eastward, shook the olive trees. A bird—a rock partridge perhaps?—yipped in the brush. The city gate creaked open and shut.

Being good at listening was often painful. Sometimes he wished he couldn't overhear his family, whispering about his future. Or the people in his village, speaking as if he weren't there. Or the religious scholars, speculating about why he was blind.

Plink, plink, plink. Bartimaeus heard the coins land in the cloak spread out in front of him. There were more people than normal outside the city today, where Bartimaeus sat in his usual spot. When he had lost his sight, he had lost his belonging as well, so he spent his days here, listening and learning.

Finally, Bartimaeus heard what he had been waiting for: a large crowd, leaving the city at once. This had to be Yeshua (Jesus) and his friends. Bartimaeus had heard a lot about Jesus. *He makes the Blind see, the Deaf hear, and the Paralyzed walk. He feeds the hungry and helps those in need.*

Almost every person passing by had a story about this mysterious new teacher. And Bartimaeus was very good at listening. Between the snippets of conversation, he heard words unsaid. *He says that impairments are not punishments! He touches the sick and visits the Disabled!*

Jesus was healing the brokenness in the ways people treated one another. He said that God's glory shone out from every body. He spoke of a new kingdom and invited everyone to belong.

Years of listening, listening, listening had left Bartimaeus with deep wisdom and discretion. And the more he heard about Jesus, the more he trusted. This was a kind man. This was a man he could follow. He *would* follow, because Bartimaeus was ready. He had a plan.

The crowd chattered and clamored as it approached, but Bartimaeus called out with all his might. "Jesus! King Jesus! Be kind to me!" He heard some shushes and grumbles, but he didn't care one bit. *What can they do? Put me even farther outside the city?* "Jesus! Jesus! Have mercy on me!" he yelled even louder, desperately hoping the stories of Jesus's kindness and power were true.

He heard the shuffling of feet grow still. The crowd had stopped moving. As Bartimaeus scrambled to stand, he heard footsteps approaching.

"This way!" came the deep rumble of one of Jesus's friends. "Take courage," came another, as sweet and melodic as a wind chime. "He's calling for you."

It was just as Bartimaeus had heard and hoped! Jesus heeded the cry of people treated as outsiders. Jesus taught people to stop and turn toward that cry. Jesus taught people to bring belonging. Bartimaeus threw his cloak to the side and heard the coins clink and scatter. He lifted his chin and hurried to Jesus.

"What would you like me to do?" Jesus's warm and steadfast voice drew near, and in his words, Bartimaeus heard the other words unsaid. *How are you suffering? What do you need? How can I show kindness to you?*

"My great teacher," Bartimaeus said breathlessly. "I want to see again."

"You trust me!" said Jesus. He knew Bartimaeus's heart. "You're saved!" continued Jesus. "Go on!"

And immediately Bartimaeus could see. The olive trees swaying in the eastward wind. The rock partridge yipping in the brush. The creaking gate to the city where he had once belonged. He knew he could walk up the path and through that gate without being stopped. He could belong again to his old life.

Go on, Jesus had said. *Go on. Go on. Go on.* But the path went the other direction as well. Jesus and his friends trudged along it now, away from the city, toward the next glimpse of heaven on earth. Bartimaeus didn't hesitate. He knew exactly where he belonged.

He hurried down the path and followed after Jesus, his great teacher.

WONDER MOMENT

WE KNOW THAT DISABLED PEOPLE BELONG WITH GOD and take part in God's dream. We see this in the stories of Jacob, Ehud, Mephibosheth, and Moses, which highlight the pride and strength in their disabilities.

Yet the Bible has many stories about Jesus healing people. Why do you think that is? Jesus cured some people to end their suffering and prevent early death, because he came to bring glimpses of heaven to earth. And in God's world, there is no suffering or death. Jesus cured other people because their lack of belonging was making them suffer. This was a trickier problem, because it had to do with other people's hearts.

Impairment doesn't always cause suffering or death. But lack of belonging *always* causes suffering and sometimes even death. In biblical days, it was a common belief that impairments and diseases were punishments for having done something wrong. Many times sick or impaired people were put outside of belonging, because they "deserved it." Does that match God's dream for blessing the world?

Think about your circles of belonging. Are people of all shapes, sizes, and abilities welcome? Is it easy to participate? Are you learning from Blind, Deaf, Disabled, and Neurodivergent friends?

If not, how can you make sure everyone belongs?

THE ONE WHO WATCHES AND WAITS

LUKE 15

Yeshua is also called Jesus.

ESHUA (JESUS) SAT, SURROUNDED CLOSELY BY THE so-called outsiders he was very fond of. But at the edges of the crowd, he heard the religious leaders grumble and groan.

"Look at him! He seeks out the sinners and even feasts with them!" They had forgotten that God's promise was to bless the whole world. They were trying to earn God's love by memorizing and following the rules. So you can imagine how they felt about rule breakers!

But Jesus knew. Jesus turned to them, his heart soft and strong, and began to tell a story.

There was a man who had two sons. When the boys were grown, the younger one came to their father and said, "I wish you were dead! Give me my inheritance!" And despite the hurtful, hateful words, his dad did exactly that: He sold half of his things and gave money and freedom to this son.

The boy immediately ran away to a far-off land and wasted the money on the type of life that does not last: hurtful, harmful living. Before long, his money was gone, so he got a job feeding pigs—filthy, disgusting work. He was hungry,

cold, and helpless. It occurred to him, *I should go home. I don't deserve to belong there, but I could still work for my father and earn some food!*

Little did he know that his father had been watching and waiting. Every morning, the father would stare at the spot where the sky met the sea, hope humming in his heart. And then—yes!—one morning he saw a shuffling shape in the distance. Immediately he knew. *That's my beloved child! I belong with him, and he belongs with me.*

And without a care as to what anyone might think or say, the father picked up his robe and ran. Crashing into his son with a hug, he kissed and held him like he would never let go.

But the son's shame pulled his gaze to the ground. He began to speak the words he had practiced, not able to look his father in the eye. "Father, I've messed up. God knows it, and so do you. I don't deserve to belong here anymore, but I was thinking—"

His father interrupted with a booming shout: "Bring rich robes! Fancy rings. Sturdy sandals. Drape my son in my belonging. Let's feast. Let's party! My child was lost and now is found. He was dead and now he's alive!"

The father pulled his child by the hand back to the home he had left behind. This sent a clear message: *You are never too far from my love. You've forgotten your name, but I never will. What you've done is not the same as who you are. I know who you are. You Belong, you are Beloved, and you Delight me.*

And so the wild rumpus began. The older son returned from the fields, stinky, sweaty, and exhausted. "What is going on?" he shouted over the music, dancing, and feasting.

"Your brother has come home, and your father threw a party to celebrate!"

Anger filled the older son, hot and sharp and heavy. It rooted him to the spot, and he refused to go inside. And when the father left the party to plead with him, his anger flashed and burned. "Look at me! Sweaty and exhausted like always. I work so hard for my belonging. I would never insult you or disobey you or leave you. But you've never thrown a party for me! And when my brother—a rule breaker! a sinner! a scoundrel!—waltzes back in, it's a feast with the whole village?"

And as the son's anger melted into sadness, which melted into fear, the father held his older son's face in his big, worn hands. "My beloved child, you have always belonged. It has nothing to do with your work. Everything I have is already yours. There's no need to earn it."

Tears soaked the older son's face, sinking in with the good words of his father: "I would leave the party to bring you in. You've forgotten your name, but I never will. Who you are doesn't depend on what you've done. I know who you are. You are Beloved, you Belong, and you Delight me.

"And now we celebrate because your brother, who was dead, is alive again. He was lost but now is found!"

Jesus finished his story and went back to his wild rumpus. At the edge of the party, the religious leaders looked at one another. Would they follow him into the celebration or stay on the outside and grumble?

A WIDE AND WIGGLING WALL

MATTHEW 18; MARK 10

Yeshua is also called Jesus.

HE CHILDREN STARED UP AT THE WALL. LIKE MOST walls, it was tall. Like most walls, it was wide. Like most walls, it got in the way of some perfectly good romping and running. But unlike most walls, this one was . . . hairy. And kind of . . . stinky. Because it wasn't really a wall at all but a group of hairy, stinky, grumpy grown-ups. Friends of Yeshua (Jesus) who were using their hairy, stinky bodies to keep the children from Jesus. *Because kids are loud and distracting,* they thought. *Because kids are not as important,* they thought.

But, as often happens, the grown-ups were wrong.

Up. Over. Under. Between. The children leaped and launched and wove and wiggled, and still the wall stood firm. But Jesus knew. His laugh rang out up and over the wall as he called to his friends, "Let them in!"

Grumbling, the wall broke apart, and the kids tumbled toward Jesus. His eyes warmed and welcomed even the shyest of the group as he crouched down to greet them. And oh, what a greeting. All the goodness of God wrapped up in a human—can you imagine how that must have felt? Kindness, peace, humor, safety, trustworthiness—all the things that are best in a person—shone out at their brightest. The kids felt their fear melt away and their wonder come alive as they stared at his eyes, which seemed to shine out the same message over and over. *You Belong. You are Beloved. You Delight me.*

And so they ran to him, full sprint, as Jesus scooped up one of the gleeful, giggling kids. "You should always welcome children just as you'd welcome me! Just as you'd welcome God!" he told his friends who had stopped complaining and couldn't help but smile. *Haven't you noticed that things are upside down in the kingdom of God? Jesus was showing them yet again. Remember to remember—this is how God always wanted it.*

The powerful, the puffed up, first in line for favors? They'll be sent to the back of the line. Those waiting on the edges, watching and learning? They'll be welcomed to the center like a hug.

Jesus motioned to the wiggling, giggling kids—climbing and clamoring—and spoke very seriously: "The kingdom of God is seeping through, and these kids know how to live in it. Watch them closely, because if you can't become more like them, you'll never learn how to live here!"

Jesus stayed with the children for a long while, making sure to spend time with each one of them. He gazed into their eyes, so full of trust, and listened to their stories, so full of imagination. He called them by their good, true names, and they answered without hesitation.

And Jesus's friends watched closely. They stared at the children, as if trying to remember what they were like when they were full of questions. When they hadn't been named by anyone but God. When worship and wonder wove together like a braid.

Grown-ups like to build walls. Walls like:

"That's not possible."

"That's too much."

"That's not important."

"They don't matter."

But here was Jesus, laughing as the children wiggled, over, under, and through. What else could the grown-ups learn from those climbing in?

32

THE SHAPE OF SADNESS

JOHN 11–12

Marta is also called Martha. Miryam is also called Mary.
Eliezer is also called Lazarus. Yeshua is also called Jesus.

L IKE ANY SIBLINGS, MARTA (MARTHA), MIRYAM (Mary), and Eliezer (Lazarus) had learned to share. Some things they shared with huffs, eye rolls, and reluctance, like sweets and forgiveness. Other things they were oh so happy to share, like chores, secrets, and their friend Yeshua (Jesus). They each loved Jesus wholly and uniquely. And Jesus loved them back, wholly and uniquely.

At least that's what they thought. Yet here were Mary and Martha, preparing for Lazarus's funeral. And Jesus was nowhere to be found. "I thought Jesus might heal him," cried Martha. "How could he stay away?"

sobbed Mary. They had sent a message to Jesus, warning him that Lazarus was very sick. Long days had passed as they waited and hoped for Jesus. Lazarus got sicker and sicker and then died.

And now, now that it was much too late, they got word that Jesus was on his way. *It's not fair. It doesn't make sense.* When they heard that Jesus was coming, Martha ran to meet him, but Mary stayed at home.

Grief comes out in many different shapes. Sometimes silence. Sometimes busyness. And sometimes, oftentimes, anger. "If you had been here, Lazarus wouldn't have died!" Martha stormed. Jesus listened as she went on, her jaw and fists clenched. "But I know it's not too late! I know God will give you whatever you ask!" she pleaded. Her hope was all tangled up with her anger and sorrow.

Jesus did not untangle the feelings. "Lazarus will live again," he said gently.

"I know that," snapped Martha. "Someday he will live again. But I'm sad now."

Jesus sat with her. How could he explain God's dream? How could he fit words around the kingdom of Already and Almost, where they had only peeks and glimpses of how things should be? "Lazarus will live because of me. Death is not the end for anyone who trusts me. Do you trust me?"

Martha looked at Jesus and felt her heart ache. Sometimes things sit side by side. Hope and sorrow. Promises and disappointment. Sickness and praise. Heaven and earth. They squish and bump together in our hearts until we ache with the stretch of it all. "I trust you," she said in spite of it all. "You're the Messiah, the Rescuer."

Eventually, Mary also came out to meet Jesus, followed by the huge crowd that had gathered to mourn Lazarus. Collapsing at Jesus's feet, Mary looked up at her dear friend. She was weary and battered. For days, waves of sorrow, hope, rage, and disbelief had swept over her again and again. But Jesus was here now, solid and silent and much too late.

"If you had been here"—she gulped down a sob—"my brother wouldn't have died!" She cried and cried and cried. Her friends and family joined her until it seemed as though their tears would soak the earth in sorrow.

Jesus felt his own heart ache, and he began to weep with them. Sometimes it is so very hard to be a human. And just because he knew the end of the story, it didn't make the messy middle go away. Death, suffering, sadness—these things didn't belong in the kingdom of heaven. But in Jesus heaven bumped against earth, hope against sorrow.

"Show me where you put him," he rasped. They all walked slowly to the tomb, trailing tears behind them. But when Jesus told

them to roll the stone away from the entrance, Martha jumped in front. "His body has been dead for four days!" Martha protested. "It's probably starting to . . . stink."

But Jesus was God in a human body. Jesus was stronger than death. "Watch and see God's glory," he told Martha, grinning through his tears. And he prayed, thanking God for sending him to earth, this messy place of hope and sorrow. And then he opened his eyes, opened his mouth, and shouted.

"Lazarus!" he called to his beloved friend, his voice echoing out beyond the mysteries of death. "Lazarus, come out here!"

Shuffle . . . shuffle . . .

Gasp!

Lazarus walked out of the tomb! Now the tears were of joy, thankfulness, and wonder. *What? Why? How?*

They had no answers, only a peek. Like the peeled-back glimpse at the river with John, Jesus had shown them again what God's kingdom was like. A kingdom with no suffering. A kingdom with no grief. A kingdom with no death.

MINDFUL MOMENT

ONE OF THE TRICKIEST THINGS ABOUT BEING A PERSON is all the big, messy feelings we carry around inside us. Sometimes it's helpful to create rituals that allow us to be with those feelings.

Lament is a special ritual that gives us a place to sit with our sadness. Let's practice lament today. Have you ever lost someone you loved? (A person? A pet?) Or something you loved? (A special toy? A dream?)

Loss fills us with sadness, and that sadness shows us just how deeply we loved. It's easy to try to fix our sadness or chase it away. But what moves it through our bodies in a healthy way is to do what Jesus, Mary, and Martha did: simply be sad.

Try putting one hand over your heart and one over your belly and take some deep belly breaths. Hold a picture in your mind of who or what you lost. Spend some time breathing as you sit with your sadness, whatever shape it takes.

- Notice how your sadness feels in your body. (Is it heavy? Hot? Wobbly? Squeezing?)
- Notice what thoughts you have and share them with God. *(It's not fair! I feel forgotten! You let me down! Why?)*
- Think about how you can show love and care to someone else when they are lamenting.
- Read Psalm 13, a very good example of lament.

A PECULIAR PARADE

MATTHEW 21; JOHN 12; LUKE 13; 19

Yeshua is also called Jesus.

HE ROCK GOATS STOPPED GRAZING TO STARE. The wild dogs trotted alongside, eager tongues lolling. The falcons circled low and curious.

The strangest procession was meandering down the road to Jerusalem. Students and scholars. Rich women in their finery. Fishermen with their stooped posture. Lepers and beggars and children and animals. All following behind Yeshua (Jesus), who walked slowly and deliberately as if the dusty road had been unrolled for his purpose alone. *But what is his purpose?*

That was the question on everyone's mind as they tramped and chattered along, like ducklings trailing their mama. "I just watched him resurrect Lazarus!" squealed a woman, her fine jewelry clinking in excitement. "Do you think he'll do more miracles?" "He's going to gather an army!" growled one man to the other, gripping an old spear. "Count me in!" "If the power machine falls, we'll belong again!" hissed one beggar to another.

For generations and generations, God's people had shared

the old stories and asked the old questions and wrestled, wondering, *Is God still with us? Is God still good? Are we still loved? What about this Roman power machine? Are we forgotten? Have we forgotten?*

Someday God would send a rescuer, the old stories said. And he will ride on a donkey into the city. He will rescue the people and create a new place of belonging. Someday God will return to the city. Someday God will free them. Someday God will bring a new kingdom to earth.

God had destroyed a power machine before, rescuing them from Pharaoh. Was Jesus the new Moses? Was this the beginning of another great rescue?

Nobody knew for sure, but when a donkey was brought to Jesus, he climbed on it, and the crowd's excitement bubbled into a frenzy. The procession continued, picking up more followers with every village they passed. The people began to sing and dance, waving palm branches and throwing

HOSANNA!

their cloaks on the road. *"Hosanna! Hosanna!"* they sang. *"Rescue us, please! Blessings to the new king!"*

A group of religious leaders hurried up to Jesus as he sat atop the donkey, calming it as the crowd surged around him. "Correct them!" they sputtered. "Hush them!" This talk of a new king would only anger the power machine.

But Jesus shrugged, dismissing them. "If the people don't cry out, then the stones will!"

And it truly felt as if the stones just might cry. The joy and expectation seeped out from the crowd until it felt as if even the trees were dancing, the rocks singing, and the clouds humming along. It seemed this strange celebration could not be contained. It tumbled and bumbled closer to the city, without any of the order or frills you might expect from a royal procession. The songs got louder, and the dust cloud grew among stomps and whirls as the ragtag crowd spilled over the road.

But if you'd have been there, if you had seen Jesus's face, you might have noticed something. Amid all the swirling celebration, Jesus was weeping. He stared at the grand city, at the center of the Promised Land, where God had promised Abraham so many years before that God would bless the whole world. Tears streamed down his face, soaking his beard. "Oh, sweet city," you may have heard him sob. "Oh, my people. You think you know what peace is and how I will bring it. You don't understand, do you?"

And they didn't understand. Do we ever fully understand what God is up to in the mix of heaven and earth? But on trudged the donkey, with its rider weeping and the crowds singing—a most peculiar parade indeed.

TABLE TURNER

MATTHEW 21; MARK 11; LUKE 19; JOHN 12

Yeshua is also called Jesus.

ITH SHOUTS AND SONGS AND SHIMMIES OF PRAISE, Yeshua's (Jesus's) peculiar parade entered the city and headed straight for the temple: God's special place of belonging. At the center of the city, it shone, bright and beautiful. Like the Garden of Eden, it was supposed to be a place of togetherness. Like the tabernacle in the desert, it was supposed to be a place of hope and healing. But on the inside, it had changed. Choice by choice, greed and grasping, the temple had become a home for the power machine.

All through the special courtyard, where people who didn't know God could be—should be!—welcomed into worship, instead there was a checkpoint in the midst of a makeshift marketplace.

Jesus saw it all, and he was angry. "This should be a house of prayer for all people, but instead it is full of thieves! It should never be difficult to belong with God!" he roared.

Grabbing the edge of a table, Jesus heaved and hoisted it up and over. *Crash!* The coins spilled and rolled as the birds flew free and oxen, sheep, and goats ran wild. It was a commotion like the temple courtyard had never seen before. So-called outsiders now spilled in, eager for healing and belonging.

I CAN ONLY AFFORD A DOVE THIS YEAR...
THE PRICE IS DOUBLE FROM LAST YEAR...
GOD WILL NEVER ACCEPT THAT GIFT.
ONE OF THESE IS GUARANTEED TO MAKE GOD HAPPY.
WHAT WAS THAT?
WOW!

Swindlers fled, embarrassed and offended. Animals romped and frolicked. And darting in and around the chaos were the children, still singing at the top of their voices, "Hosanna! Hosanna! Hosanna to the king!"

I'm sure you can guess how this made the religious leaders feel. The leaders Jesus was shouting at. The leaders who were supposed to create welcome and belonging. The leaders who set up the marketplace and got rich from its business. The leaders who kept the people they considered outsiders out and corruption in. The leaders whose power and order were threatened by Jesus and his ragtag parade.

"Do you hear what these children are saying?" they blustered.

Jesus looked around at the jolly jumble and smiled. "Yes! Haven't you read your scriptures? They say that out of the mouths of children and even babies will come the sounds of strength—to silence the corrupt."

The religious leaders frowned and whispered, "He must be stopped."

Fear filled their hearts, and their thoughts turned dark and dangerous. A plan began to take shape. A plan to kill Jesus.

Then, slowly, silence filled the temple once again as the echoes of praise and justice and belonging followed Jesus out the door and wherever he went. They were the sounds of his kingdom crashing in.

MINDFUL MOMENT

OF ALL THE FEELINGS GOD GAVE US, ANGER IS ONE
of the least comfortable. It can make us feel hot, out of control,
tearful, and even scared. It's easy to feel like anger is bad. Like
when we are angry, *we* are bad.

It's comforting to remember that Jesus felt all the same
feelings we do, even anger! Anger is so important. It shows us
what we care about. It gives us energy to make things right.
When we control it, anger can help us bless the world.

Think of the last time you felt angry. Where did you feel it in
your body? How did you want to move? What does your anger
tell you is important to you?

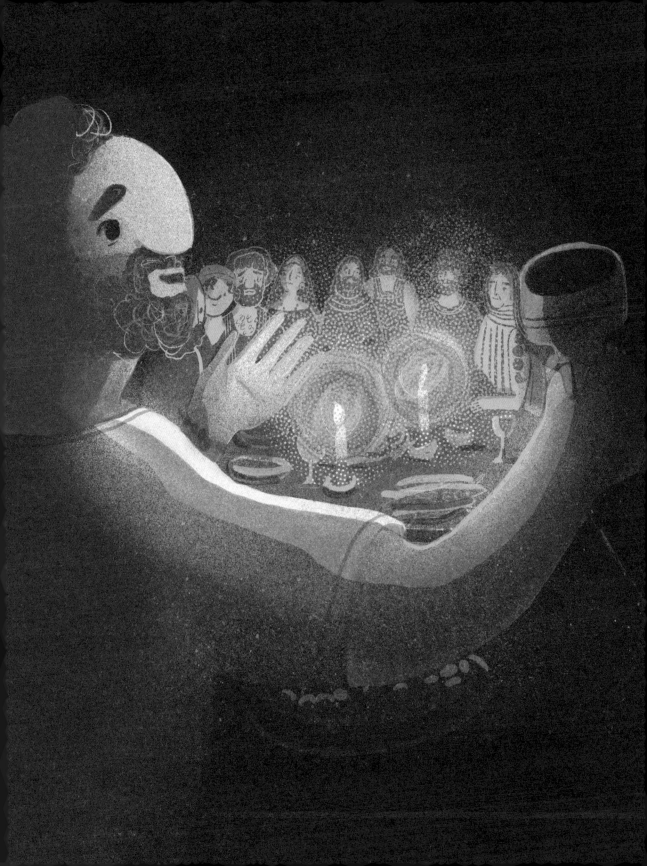

A FEAST WITH FRIENDS

MATTHEW 26; MARK 14; LUKE 22; JOHN 13; 16; 1 CORINTHIANS 11

Yeshua is also called Jesus.

HE AIR FELT HEAVY AND EXPECTANT, AS IF THE room were holding its breath. Yeshua (Jesus) sat at the table with his friends, chatting quietly in the glow of the candles. Passover was usually a lively holiday for remembering and celebrating how God rescued God's people from Egypt's power machine. The city swelled with people and parties. There were stories, songs, and cheer. But this year, in this room, it felt different.

Jesus stood with bread in hand. His friends waited for him to recite the traditional Passover words. But he surprised them all. Instead, he said a blessing, broke the bread, and handed it to them, saying, "This is like my body. Soon it is going to break." Lifting his cup, Jesus went on: "And this is like my blood. Soon it is going to pour out."

His friends were sad and confused. *Breaking bodies? Pouring blood?* Passover was supposed to be fun! A time to celebrate rescue and freedom! They didn't understand yet that in his own way, Jesus *was* celebrating rescue and freedom. Something new was happening that only Jesus understood. Just like the escape from Egypt so many centuries before, God was going to lead people to freedom and belong with them in a new way. Jesus understood that this was something worth celebrating.

Yet in some mysterious way, the suffering of Jesus's human body was going to be part of the rescue story. Like a mother who labors and cries

when she gives birth, Jesus was about to bring forth something new. And it was going to hurt. Jesus understood that this was something worth honoring. "When you break bread and sip wine, when you sit back from the table with a full heart and feel something of heaven in your gathering, remember me," Jesus told them.

Sometimes things happen that are so important and mysterious that we simply can't fit them into our human heads and hearts. They weigh us down like big, heavy stones as we puzzle and wrestle. It helps to do something with our hands and our time, to give those big feelings a place to rest. We call that a ceremony.

Jesus was giving his friends the gift of a remembering ceremony before they even knew they would need it. Something was about to happen that would change the world forever. It would confuse and inspire humans for the rest of history. Jesus didn't give his friends an explanation or a lesson; he just gave them a ceremony. A place to put their sadness, confusion, doubt, awe, and gratitude.

Jesus looked around the table at his friends. Oh, how he loved them fiercely. And he would love them right up until the end. He was making a love promise to his friends, one that he wanted them to remember in their gatherings.

Remember to remember to remember.

Like Moses sending God's people into the Promised Land, Jesus was getting his disciples ready to live in a new type of world. A rescued world. A world without him.

Jesus had one last meal with his dear friends, and he spent it in the most important way: reminding them of the truest and most beautiful things. "Love one another," he said as he washed their feet like a servant. "The way you love and care for one another will show people that you love me." He hugged them and reminded them of all he had taught, saying, "If you love me, you'll follow my teachings."

He spoke familiar words from Moses, from the Psalms, from the ancient truth-tellers, because people change but God never does. "I Belong with you, and you Belong with me. You're my Beloved. You are a Delight. Be a blessing. Take courage. Choose life and flourishing."

But he said new things as well. Things that warmed their hearts with wonder. "I'm going away soon. I'm going to prepare a new place for you, with God! I will come back to welcome you there. But I would never leave you alone. I will send a special comforter to you. A Spirit that will remind you of your true names and give you power to live in God's kingdom."

Like all special nights, time stretched out in order to make space for all the important words that needed to be said. The candlelight flickered and dimmed. The shadows grew long. Full of feast, full of fondness, full of expectation and mystery, Jesus's friends all leaned back in their chairs. Cups were tilted and voices raised as they sang one last song together, the words both familiar and strange. Then, out into the night, they walked together to the olive grove to wait and pray.

Wait for what? Only Jesus seemed to know.

36

THE
MESSY MIDDLE

MATTHEW 27; MARK 15; LUKE 23; JOHN 19

Yeshua is also called Jesus.

HAT HAPPENED NEXT WAS SO VERY DARK AND heavy but so very important. It's the part of the story we might like to skip over. Or perhaps we just cover our eyes and peek through our fingers. It shows us the very worst things in human hearts, all at once. Pride, greed, fear, shame, ignorance, and violence—they all met together with a horrible clash, like a great boom of thunder.

It began in a garden, as a great many important things do. Yeshua (Jesus), heaven and earth bound up in a body, the God who came to be a human, was sad, because even when you know the end of the story, it doesn't make the messy middle go away. His friends had fallen asleep while he prayed, and the olive grove was dark and lonesome. He talked with God, sharing his big feelings and asking for comfort, courage, and direction. And God was with him.

And then they came to get him. Men with torches and weapons, sneaking through the night, people who had something to hide. Priests, temple guards, religious leaders, armed like soldiers. It was all so backward and wrong. "No violence," Jesus told his friends, who were awake now, ready to fight. "Put your swords away." And then he turned to the men, looking them in the eyes. "Am I so dangerous that you've brought swords and clubs to collect me? You know me. You've been with me in the temple every day, but you didn't lay a finger on me."

But that was the day, and this was the night. And under the cover of darkness, the religious leaders were led by fear. They grasped for control. They grabbed Jesus and took him to the house of the head priest, a man corrupted by power. They questioned Jesus and mocked him and plotted and schemed. Then they sent him to Pilate and Herod, leaders in the Roman power machine.

Did they know the full story of who they were looking at? Do we ever really know the full story of who we are looking at?

"He talks about a new kingdom, but we already have a king!" the Roman leaders claimed. "He is not loyal to our power machine!"

"He breaks the rules. He threatens the peace and says he is the new place of belonging with God!" the religious leaders agreed. "He is not loyal to our traditions!"

*He's not loyal. **He's dangerous. He needs to be stopped.*** They decided that Jesus would be crucified. Executed like a traitor.

It was a horrible day, and Jesus felt every horrible thing a human could ever feel. His body was used and abused so that people in power could keep feeling powerful. And then he was hung on a cross of wood.

He felt alone. He felt abandoned. But he didn't fight back. He didn't escape. He was God in a body, and that body was part of a bigger story. A story of heaven bumping earth. Hope mixing with sorrow. A story of Already and Almost. So there he hung in the messy

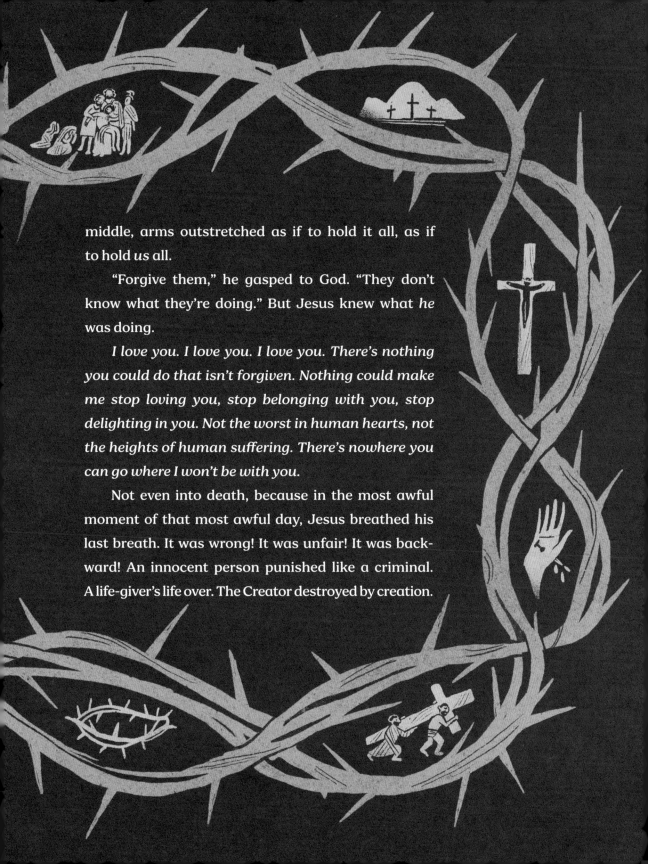

middle, arms outstretched as if to hold it all, as if to hold *us* all.

"Forgive them," he gasped to God. "They don't know what they're doing." But Jesus knew what *he* was doing.

I love you. I love you. I love you. There's nothing you could do that isn't forgiven. Nothing could make me stop loving you, stop belonging with you, stop delighting in you. Not the worst in human hearts, not the heights of human suffering. There's nowhere you can go where I won't be with you.

Not even into death, because in the most awful moment of that most awful day, Jesus breathed his last breath. It was wrong! It was unfair! It was back-ward! An innocent person punished like a criminal. A life-giver's life over. The Creator destroyed by creation.

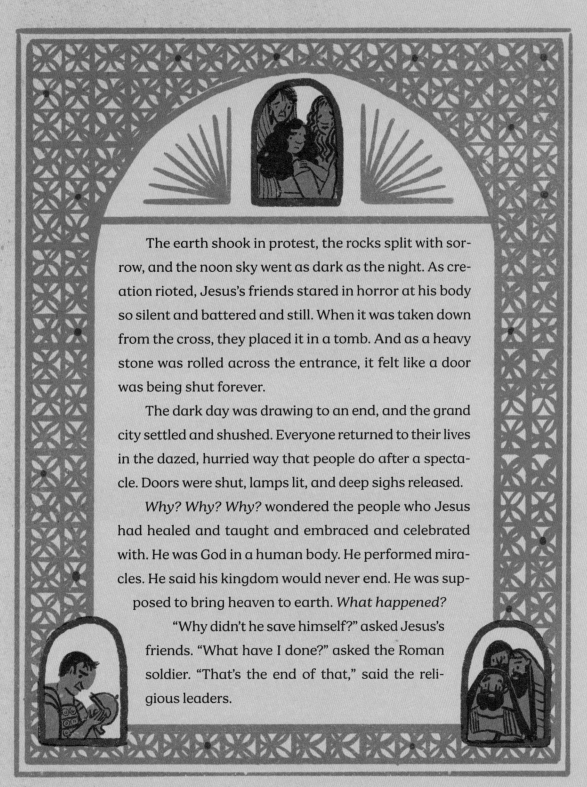

The earth shook in protest, the rocks split with sorrow, and the noon sky went as dark as the night. As creation rioted, Jesus's friends stared in horror at his body so silent and battered and still. When it was taken down from the cross, they placed it in a tomb. And as a heavy stone was rolled across the entrance, it felt like a door was being shut forever.

The dark day was drawing to an end, and the grand city settled and shushed. Everyone returned to their lives in the dazed, hurried way that people do after a spectacle. Doors were shut, lamps lit, and deep sighs released.

Why? Why? Why? wondered the people who Jesus had healed and taught and embraced and celebrated with. He was God in a human body. He performed miracles. He said his kingdom would never end. He was supposed to bring heaven to earth. *What happened?*

"Why didn't he save himself?" asked Jesus's friends. "What have I done?" asked the Roman soldier. "That's the end of that," said the religious leaders.

Because although death was a mystery,
most people would agree that it was the end.

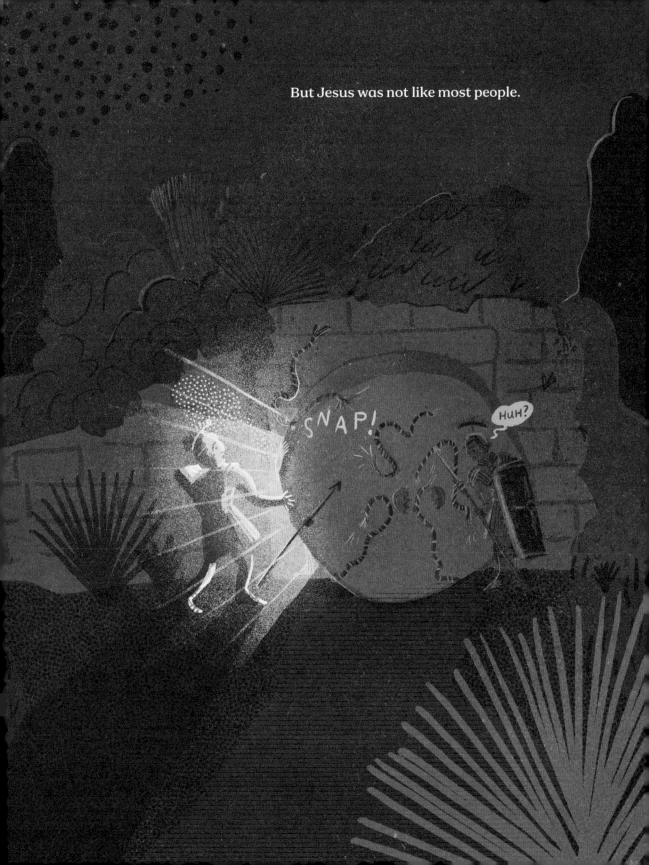

A SURPRISE VISITOR

MATTHEW 28; MARK 16; LUKE 24; JOHN 20

Miryam the Migdal is also called Mary Magdalene. Yokhana is also called Joanna. Shlomit is also called Salome. Yeshua is also called Jesus.

T WAS SO EARLY THE SUN WAS STILL ASLEEP. THE air was dark and heavy. Miryam the Migdal's (Mary Magdalene's) heart felt heavy too. Cold dew tickled and trickled along her ankles as she and her friends moved through the garden toward Yeshua's (Jesus's) tomb, carrying spices to prepare his body.

"Okay, here's the plan," she whispered. "I'll pull from the front, and you two push from the back." "Pull?" Yokhana (Joanna) said, laughing and wiping her eyes. "My friend, you are strong, but even you can't pull a stone that size."

Shlomit (Salome) and the other women looked on, speechless in their grief. It was Sunday morning and Jesus had been dead since Friday

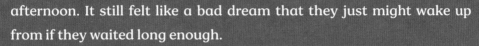

afternoon. It still felt like a bad dream that they just might wake up from if they waited long enough.

Rounding the corner, Mary Magdalene stopped so abruptly that the women slammed into one another: *bonk, bonk, bonk.*

What a bizarre sight to behold. The heavy stone was rolled away from the entrance of Jesus's tomb, and on top of it perched a . . . Someone. Was it an angel? Was it a person? The Someone shone like lightning in a robe of blazing white. And flopped on the ground beneath the Someone lay Roman soldiers. They had been sent to guard Jesus's tomb, but they had fainted at the sight.

Mary Magdalene thought she just might faint as well. But she felt her friends behind her and heard the Someone's reassuring voice saying, "Don't be alarmed. I know you're looking for Jesus, who was killed.

He's not here—he is alive again. He told you this would happen!"

He's not here? He's alive again? It was impossible, wasn't it? They had watched Jesus suffer and die. They had seen his battered body being laid in this tomb. But here was this Someone, telling them a pretty incredible Something. It made the women question what *impossible* might really mean.

They had watched Jesus calm storms with his words. They had watched him heal diseases and multiply food and repair broken families and systems and hearts. He was so much bigger and brighter than their rules and words and beliefs. Was it so impossible that he was bigger than death too? So with whoops and wails of wonder, the women hurried off. *He's not here! He's alive again!*

But Mary Magdalene trailed behind, crying and crying, a storm of feelings building in her mighty heart. Grief, joy, confusion, awe. "Why are you crying? Who are you looking for?" came a voice, jolly and gentle and oh so familiar. She turned, squinting against the first rays of rising sun, and saw a man. *Who else would be in the garden this early? A gardener perhaps?*

"I'm looking for Jesus," she said as her heart thumped and jumped.

"Mary!" came the voice again, and this time she knew. Is there a better feeling in the world than someone you love calling your name? Gladness filled her from head to toe as she shouted out, "My teacher!" and flung herself at Jesus. Because of course it was Jesus. Of course he was alive. It had seemed impossible, but if her good teacher had taught her anything, it was that nothing is impossible with God.

Mary clung to her friend. The bad dream was over, and Jesus's aliveness made all her other fears and worries slide away like shadows being chased off by sunshine. Death was not the end. What other impossible things were possible?

The sun rose and the birds trilled and Jesus laughed. "It's time to let go, Mary! Go and tell my friends that I'm alive!"

What could she do but obey? Mary went out from the garden, her grin splitting wide open. Every story Jesus had ever told her, every true name he had ever called her, all played like a lovely song in the back of her mind. Something new was happening. Something wild and mysterious and so very good. Back in the city, surrounded by Jesus's friends and students, Mary—tower of truth—stood tall and shouted the best truth she had ever known:

"Jesus is risen! He is risen indeed!"

A DREAM COME TRUE

MATTHEW 28; MARK 16; LUKE 24; JOHN 20; ACTS 1

Yeshua is also called Jesus.
Miryam the Migdal is also called Mary Magdalene

ESHUA'S (JESUS'S) FRIENDS questioned Miryam the Migdal (Mary Magdalene) and the other women: "How can this be?"

"What does it mean?"

"Who?"

"What?"

"Why?"

Who better to ask than Jesus himself, who visited many of them over the next few weeks. He hugged them and feasted with them. He took walks and taught them about the scriptures. He fished with them and made them breakfast.

Can you imagine the joy and amazement they felt? How could they believe what they were seeing? How could they *not* believe?

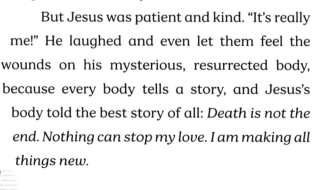

But Jesus was patient and kind. "It's really me!" He laughed and even let them feel the wounds on his mysterious, resurrected body, because every body tells a story, and Jesus's body told the best story of all: *Death is not the end. Nothing can stop my love. I am making all things new.*

Jesus was showing them what it looks like when God's dream comes true.

After they spent many joyous days together, he led them outside the city. Lifting up his scarred hands, which they had seen spread wide to embrace the whole world, he told them many true and beautiful things. He looked in their eyes and reminded them of God's true names for them: Beloved, Belonging, and Delightful. "This has all been part of God's dream of belonging coming true. I want you to share that dream with the whole world!"

Jesus's friends looked at one another and then back at their teacher. There was a bittersweet ache in their throats, and they couldn't quite say why.

HEAVEN WAS OPEN.

And then something lovely happened: It wasn't the first time, and it wouldn't be the last, but it was as if the world around them split open. The swaying grasses and dancing clouds peeled back to show a glimpse of heaven: God's world. Like a grin breaking open with joy, like a door creaking to reveal a room full of wonders. Light and love poured out, and somehow Jesus entered in.

He left them and was taken into God's space.

Jesus's friends blinked and stared at the place where their beloved friend and teacher and rescuer had just been standing. Did they know the whole story of who they had been looking at? Do we ever really know the whole story of who we are looking at?

In the same, simple way God had slipped into the world, in the form of a baby born to the most ordinary of girls, God was changing everything through Jesus, and nobody had even realized it. Something bright and kind and beautiful was shifting in the universe and in human hearts forever.

It was like a door swung open that they didn't know had been keeping them trapped. It was like someone paid for a huge bill that they couldn't afford. It was like Jesus got in a fight with death and he won. It was like Jesus had showed them how to live and love but now was leaving so they could practice on their own.

None of our words seem quite magnificent enough to describe the mystery of what was happening in the kingdom of Already and Almost.

Without warning, something bright and warm bubbled up in each of them. It spread and soothed their aching hearts and racing minds. It was joy. A great big bubble of joy that seemed to carry them above the road as they made their way back to the city.

Jesus was alive. Heaven was open.

Something new was happening, and they got to be part of it.

A WIND IN THE DOOR

ACTS 2

Shavuot is also called Pentecost. Petros is also called Peter.
Yeshua is also called Jesus.

T IS SO DIFFICULT TO WAIT. IT IS EVEN MORE difficult when you're waiting on a mystery visitor. But that's what Yeshua's (Jesus's) friends were doing up there in the cramped and crowded room: waiting. Jesus had told them not to leave the city because God would send them a helper called the Holy Spirit. *How exactly?* No clue. *When exactly?* No idea.

So as the city swelled with visitors, in town for the thanksgiving festival of Shavuot (Pentecost), they waited. Watching the gate. Scanning the streets. Through the feast and the frivolity of the Pentecost celebrations. Chewing nails. Drumming fingers. They came; they went; they waited.

And then, without warning, a wind came through the door. It was thunderous and refreshing, blustering like seaside swells. It filled the room; it filled their ears; it filled their hearts. As their hair stood on end, they looked around the room and watched one another's eyes and mouths grow round with wonder.

And then, like fireflies dancing across the meadow, like stars that twinkle, steadfast, like lamplight that welcomes you home, a Light shimmered into the room, separating to rest on each of them, setting them aglow. It was the Holy Spirit—their promised visitor. It made them feel warm and glad and energized.

True and beautiful words began to tumble out of their mouths as they all began to talk at once. They grew louder and gladder, spilling into the street, where a crowd had gathered to investigate the commotion. The crowd was made up of people who had traveled to Jerusalem from places as far as Europe, Asia, and Africa, yet they were each astonished to hear Jesus's friends speaking in their own languages as they whooped and whirled and shared about God's wonders. *But these people are not from our lands! They don't speak our language! This is not possible!*

There were cheers and jeers. Marveling and mocking. But Petros (Peter), wild and windswept, couldn't keep quiet. He knew what was happening. He recognized the shimmer of belonging that marked so many of their sacred stories. The same fire had greeted God's people at Sinai. The same glow had settled on the tabernacle, gleaming at the center of their wilderness camp. It had filled the temple, lighting the way for the kings and queens of Israel. It had spilled over from heaven as Jesus was baptized, God's good names settling on him like a dove.

And now God's Spirit was with them in a new way. God's dream was coming true! God's kingdom was spilling in! So Peter took a deep breath and began to tell the story of Jesus in the way that only Peter could. He had seen it all. *I am who he says I am. Jesus is who he says he is.* He wove together the wonderful story of how Jesus lived and loved and died and rose. "Don't you see?" Peter cried out. "Jesus is the Rescuer, the Messiah! The one to make all things new!" This was good news indeed. Then, just as Jesus had dunked under the water, rose, and received God's Spirit, many people rushed forward to be baptized as well. Three thousand people trusted in God's dream for them.

And just like Jesus had promised, the Holy Spirit became their helper, so they could live and love as Jesus had. Throughout the city, they feasted with the forgotten and shared with anyone in need, even selling their possessions to give money to the poor. They healed, studied, and welcomed others into belonging.

At some point, the mysterious Light faded. But like a silhouette that's visible even when you close your eyes, God's people never forgot. Like fireflies dancing across the meadow, like stars that twinkle, steadfast, like lamplight that welcomes you home, the Spirit shone in their eyes and words and deeds, declaring, "There is life and flourishing here. This is a place of belonging."

The Pentecost festival came to an end, and the celebrators trekked home, some to nearby villages and some farther on to Africa, Asia, and Europe. Some carried the Spirit within, a steady glow. God's kingdom had spilled in, and now it spread out to light up the whole world, just as God dreamed, just as Jesus had promised.

MINDFUL MOMENT

WHOOOOOOOOOSH. THE OLDEST BIBLE STORIES ARE written in Hebrew and Greek. The Hebrew word for Spirit is *ruakh* (ROO-akh). The Greek word for Spirit is *pneuma* (NOOM-ah). Both of these words can also mean "wind" or "breath."

Why do you think they chose these words?

Wind is invisible.

Breath keeps us alive.

Wind can be powerful or soothing.

A deep breath brings us peace and clarity.

Wind is around us.

Breath is within us.

Spend some time outside today, noticing the wind and noticing your breath. How do your observations help you understand God's Spirit?

CROWDED TABLES
OF KINDNESS

ACTS 12; PHILIPPIANS; COLOSSIANS

Rhode is also called Rhoda. Yokhana is also called Joanna.
Miryam is also called Mary. Reuven is also called Reuben.
Yeshua is also called Jesus.

THE DONKEY'S TAIL GREW LONGER AND WISPIER until it disappeared altogether. Rhode (Rhoda) watched, fascinated, as the donkey slowly rolled away, chased by a . . . giant rabbit . . . with a . . . sword! *Knock knock knock.*

Rhoda jumped away from the window, where she had been cloud gazing again. There was someone at the door, and as unofficial Guardian of the Door, Rhoda took her job very seriously. *Who is it this time?* she wondered as she hurried down the stairs on her tiny feet. *Maybe a donkey with no tail or a rabbit with a sword,* she thought, giggling to herself.

When Rhoda had first come to work there, it was quiet. A grand house with echoing, empty rooms and a solid, silent door. Miryam (Mary), woman of the house, was often away, traveling with Yeshua's (Jesus's) friends or off to the temple, leaving Rhoda to her cloud watching and daydreaming. It was a bit lonely.

But so much had happened recently, and the door had been very busy with a peculiar mix of people knocking. And every person who passed through the door had another story to tell.

Knock knock.

"Jesus was killed! It was gruesome!" said Yokhana (Joanna) as she swept through in her fancy robes.

Knock knock knock .

"But he's alive again!" Miryam the Migdal (Mary Magdalene) grinned. "He called my name!"

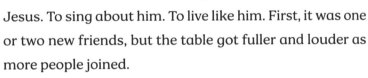

Knock. Knock knock knock.

"And God's Spirit is now with the people!" cheered Reuven (Reuben), a worker from the docks.

Rhoda, Guardian of the Door and Watcher of the Clouds, heard it all. *But why are you all here?* she wondered at first.

As weeks passed, it became obvious: They were there to talk about

Jesus. To sing about him. To live like him. First, it was one or two new friends, but the table got fuller and louder as more people joined.

They all sat together: enslaved humans, old humans, rich humans, poor humans. They shared everything they had, making sure no one went hungry or needed shelter. They clanked their cups against hers and sang songs about forgiveness. They read letters from their teachers and debated loudly into the night about love and power and death and new life.

But not everybody was excited to talk about Jesus. Soon the same powerful people who had him killed began trying to stop anyone who shared about him. They even threw some of Jesus's friends in prison.

Rhoda considered all this as she made her way to the door. What was on the other side? Was it another friend? Was it trouble?

Knock knock knock.

"Hello? Hello?" a low voice called out.

Rhoda froze, staring at the door. She may often have her head in the clouds, but she had deep knowing in her heart. And she recognized that voice. It was Petros (Peter)! Friend of Jesus, preacher, teacher, and leader. He was supposed to be in prison! Their friends would be so overjoyed!

And maybe it was the excitement, maybe it was the shock, or maybe it was the clouds, but Rhoda, Guardian of the Door, dashed away, leaving Peter outside, knocking. Rhoda hurried through the house, tripping and skipping, arriving breathlessly beside the crowded dining table. "Sit, Rhoda, sit!" the group called, as they always did. This was still new and strange. Rhoda was used to serving and working. She stayed silent and out of the way. She stayed separate.

But these Jesus followers welcomed all to their table. And what a jolly table it was. "I can't sit! Peter is at the door!" Rhoda cried. But they didn't believe her. "Silly girl, Peter is in prison! You must be dreaming again!"

But Rhoda trusted herself. "It's Peter! I know it is!"

Knock knock knock.

This time, they all heard it. And like so many clumsy clouds, rolling and bumping together, they all tumbled toward the door.

Servants and merchants and children and priests. But Rhoda got there first, flinging it wide. There stood Peter, full of stories to tell.

Peter always brought news and letters from other Jesus followers at other crowded tables in other cities near and far. Like vines creeping up a tree, like spilled wine seeping across cloth, like a blush of sunrise stealing across the horizon, word about Jesus and the good news of his upside-down, inside-out kingdom had spread quickly and permanently. And Peter had seen it all, going from table to table crowded with humans bent on kindness, justice, forgiveness, and learning.

At the door, they all clamored and cheered, reaching to welcome Peter inside. But he gestured wildly, shushing them. "Quiet down!"

In a whisper, he told them a marvelous story about how an angel had freed him from prison and led him through the city streets. Rhoda stared and stared as her imagination gathered and rolled, forming pictures to match the story.

"I have to go. They'll be looking for me," Peter whispered. He turned to Rhoda. "Tell my story to all the other women and men too!" he said, crouching to meet her wide and watchful eyes. Rhoda nodded, looking serious. And then he was gone, disappearing into the night like the wisp of a cloud.

The grand house was quiet for a moment, and then Rhoda shut the door. Everyone bumbled back to the table. "Sit, Rhoda, sit!" they said, as they always did. And so she sat.

As they ate and prayed and sang and talked, Rhoda's wide and watchful eyes traveled over the faces gathered around. Old, young, clean, dirty, well kept, well worn. She knew these faces. She knew their stories. She knew what drew them together and kept them moving forward.

This Jesus person had lived, loved, died, and rose so people like them could gather like this. Each different, each changing, each moving on mission like clouds across the horizon.

MINDFUL MOMENT

THE BIBLE INCLUDES MANY STORIES THAT WOULD typically not have been told in that time period. Stories like Rhoda's! But even in the Bible, Rhoda's story is told in only a few sentences, leaving our imaginations to fill in the details.

We know from the Bible and from historical documents that early churches often met in people's homes. We know that they shared with one another and didn't separate between rich and poor or women and men.

But history is recorded by those who can record. In those days, that would have been mostly rich, educated men. So most of what we have are their stories. But what about other people like Rhoda? Many of the gatherings and events described in the Bible would have been possible only because of a crew of enslaved people, servants, and household employees working hard in the background. Their stories are mostly left untold.

So anytime we read a story from the Bible (or anywhere!), it is a helpful practice to ask ourselves, *Whose story is not being told?* This is a chance to use our imaginations in a holy and compassionate way.

THE PURVEYOR OF PURPLE

ACTS 16

*Paulos is also called Paul. Shila is also called Silas or Silvanus.
Philippos is also called Philip. Kornelios is also called Cornelius.
Prisca is also called Priscilla. Akylas is also called Aquila.
Iounia is also called Junia. Andronikos is also called Andronicus.
Loidi is also called Lois. Eunike is also called Eunice. Timotheos
is also called Timothy. Titos is also called Titus.*

YDIA'S FINGERNAILS WERE ALWAYS PURPLE. Shades of lilac, lavender, aubergine, and plum. Though she scrubbed and scrubbed, the color never quite came off. She glanced up from her purplish hands, across the piles of fabric on her worktable to her new, mysterious friends.

She had met Paulos (Paul) and Shila (Silas) just a few hours before at the riverside. She often gathered there with a group of other women to pray before she started her day, selling purple cloth in the marketplace. The two men had approached, explaining that they were visiting Philippi all the way

from Jerusalem. They had seen the women in prayer and began to talk excitedly about God. Lydia knew their God, but then they began to talk about Yeshua (Jesus) the Rescuer and all that he had done. Lydia listened carefully, asking many questions.

"I spend my days in business with rich and important people," she said. "I know a person with authority when I see one." If what these men said was true, then God was blessing the whole world through the Spirit and everyone was welcome. Lydia and her family became Jesus followers, dunking under the water to celebrate their new lives.

But Lydia knew that words about belonging were just the beginning. Were Paul and Silas ready to fully welcome her, a foreigner? "If God's kingdom is already here—and those of us treated as outsiders are welcomed in—prove it. Come and stay at my house," Lydia had challenged.

And here they were. The sun threw shadows across the room as Lydia gestured with her stained fingers. "Tell me more about what's happening," she urged the two men. "Why have you traveled so far?"

Paul leaned back against the wall and let the memories play across the backs of his eyelids. What a full life he had lived. What horrible and wonderful things he had done. What a powerful and mysterious God who had called and carried him through. Scholarly debates. Shipwrecks. Earthquakes. Angels. Miracles. And Paul knew that God would continue to carry him through adventures and difficulties to come. Down the curling, dusty ribbon of road, carrying him from one end of the kingdom to the other. From one crowded table of kindness to the next. "God's family is growing," he finally said. And he told her about God's friends, all over the map.

There's Philippos, also called Philip the Evangelist. He's traveled everywhere, talking about Jesus, but now he serves the poor in Jerusalem. He has four daughters, and each one of them is a prophet! You should hear Philip's story about the time he met a friend who worked for the queen of Ethiopia! They read the Bible together, the friend was baptized, and now there are Jesus followers in Africa!

Kornelios (Cornelius) is a leader in the Roman army. He was part of the power machine, but the kingdom that Jesus brought is for everyone. He decided to follow Jesus, and the Holy Spirit is with him now too!

Prisca and Akylas (Priscilla and Aquila) are tentmakers and teachers of truth who sailed with me on some of my adventures. They've risked their lives for me!

I can't forget about Iounia (Junia) and Andronikos (Andronicus). They were in prison with me! And Eunike (Eunice) and Loidi (Lois). They taught my friend Timotheos (Timothy) everything he knows about God. After all, they are his mother and grandmother. My former student Titos (Titus) leads the church way over on the island of Crete!

Paul continued to share stories about God's friends all over the map. From Philemon's house in Colossae to Nympha's gatherings in Laodicea to Priscilla and Aquila's table in Rome. And on and on at the tables of Phoebe, Chloe, and Apphia. Into homes in Syria, Turkey, Asia, and now here in Philippi, the very edge of Europe.

By the time Paul finished talking, his eyes were full of tears. Each journey had been a lesson. Each crowded table had been a gift. He turned to Lydia and explained, "Some of these friends are like me. They grew up with God, knew all the old stories and rules. Some of them are like you: They are new to God's family and new to God's ways. But didn't I tell you? God's family is growing." Lydia grinned as Paul continued.

"I tried to stop it at first. I thought the kingdom of God belonged only with Israel. But God changed my mind and opened my heart. God showed me that everyone belongs, and now I spend my life doing what Jesus did: inviting people into that belonging.

"Men and women. Insiders and outsiders. Powerful and powerless. God has always belonged with us, and we have always belonged with God. First in a garden, then a family, then a tent, then a kingdom, then in Jesus, and now in human hearts everywhere. God is blessing the whole world, and we get to be part of it!"

Lydia and her family talked with Paul and Silas late into the night, and they became fast friends. Soon, Lydia's grand house became home to its own crowded table of Jesus followers. Like the dye that stained her fingers purple, the good news of Jesus was seeping, permanent. It marked her, changed her, made everything different. Her power and influence helped it spread from her table, throughout her city, and to other communities in Europe. God's family was growing, God's Spirit was present and powerful, and God's kingdom could not be stopped. It welcomed and wove like a tapestry more lavish and beautiful than anyone could have imagined.

WONDER MOMENT

WHAT WERE CHURCHES LIKE IN THOSE EARLY DAYS? Who was in charge? What songs did they sing? What exactly did they think of Jesus? What rules did they have? Our answers are mostly guesses.

Most of what we know about people who believed and preached the good news of Jesus comes from ancient letters to churches in cities all over Asia Minor, Eastern Europe, and the Middle East. That's right—from reading other people's mail!

Many of the letters seem to be written by Paul, and some by Peter, John, and Yaakov (also called James). Some were written by mystery people, and we can merely make guesses at who they were.

Since we are peeking in on someone else's mail, we can gather only bits and pieces about what was important to that specific group of people at that time. They weren't writing to record history; they were writing to talk to friends and share wise lessons. (In fact, the story before and after this Wonder Moment comes from those letters!)

I wonder what details we've missed. I wonder whose stories aren't being told. I wonder what future people might assume about our churches from the letters we write!

A FOREVER WEDDING FEAST

REVELATION

Yokhanan is also called John. Yeshua is also called Jesus.

OD'S FAMILY CONTINUED TO GROW, AND MANY marvelous and terrible things happened. Things you'd learn today as ancient history. There were art, medicine, and architecture, but there were also wars and earthquakes and volcanoes and suffering. The Roman power machine grew, and God's people continued to be in danger.

And in the midst of all this hope and suffering were Yeshua's (Jesus's) friends. Telling his story, living like he did, and trusting that God's dream for them was good and growing. One of those friends—Yokhanan (John)—wrote a letter to some of Jesus's followers, describing a vision that God showed him. A daydream of sorts.

You know how dreams are: weird and wonderful. Sometimes they feel scary, and sometimes they feel silly. But every once in a while, they feel very special. Have you ever had a dream like that? One that feels more true than real life and when you try to explain it to someone else, your words just don't seem big enough, so you can only say, "It was kind of like . . ." or "It was sort of like . . ." or "It reminded me of . . ."?

That's the kind of daydream John had. Though with all the earthquakes and dragons and beasts at its start, some people might call it a nightmare. John's awake life had showed him that the world can feel dark and weird and scary. Perhaps it had seeped into his dream, as our awake life does with *our* dreams.

It was kind of like . . . It was sort of like . . .
Flaming horses and creatures covered in eyeballs.

A red moon and falling stars.

Lions breathing fire, and bugs wearing crowns.

But the Spirit reminded John that God's dream is always coming true. So if the story doesn't end in belonging, the story is not over. Sure enough, John's daydream began to change as the strange and scary gave way to something beautiful. John saw Jesus ride in on a white horse, defeating the dragons and beasts, removing evil kings from their thrones, and chasing away all the darkness and sorrow and fear.

Then, at the end of this bizarre and beautiful daydream, John described seeing a glimpse of a big, important *someday.* The day when God's world and our world mix together once and for all. When God's kingdom will spill out as if from a giant bowl, splashing to fill the earth.

And what a spectacular sight he tried to describe, as the whole world became God's ultimate place of belonging. *It was kind of like . . . It was sort of like . . .*

Something like a city with streets like transparent gold and walls like sparkling gemstones and jewels! A river runs through the center, surrounded by a magnificent tree of life! The tree has twelve different kinds of fruit and leaves that will heal the whole world! The gates are like giant pearls

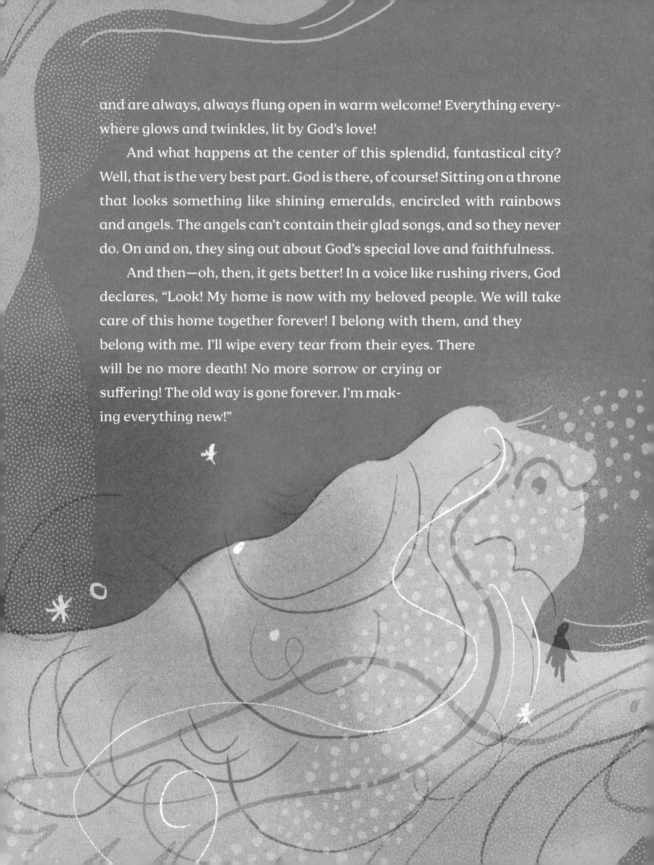

and are always, always flung open in warm welcome! Everything everywhere glows and twinkles, lit by God's love!

And what happens at the center of this splendid, fantastical city? Well, that is the very best part. God is there, of course! Sitting on a throne that looks something like shining emeralds, encircled with rainbows and angels. The angels can't contain their glad songs, and so they never do. On and on, they sing out about God's special love and faithfulness.

And then—oh, then, it gets better! In a voice like rushing rivers, God declares, "Look! My home is now with my beloved people. We will take care of this home together forever! I belong with them, and they belong with me. I'll wipe every tear from their eyes. There will be no more death! No more sorrow or crying or suffering! The old way is gone forever. I'm making everything new!"

Can you hear it? Can you see it? Can you imagine?

And then John says he saw what it will be like, when God meets together with God's people at last in their forever home. Out of all the bright and beautiful words and pictures John could have used ("sort of like . . . ," "kind of like . . ."), John said this:

It will be like a wedding feast! A never-ending table stretching past the horizons. And all the seats will be filled with friends from every tribe and language and people and nation. Togetherness! Celebration! Songs and cheers! True and beautiful names proclaimed. Important promises made and kept.

All the very best things about love and parties and weddings and feasts—we love them because they remind us of this forever belonging that is God's dream. Doesn't this just fill your heart and imagination right up to the brim? Is there anything more important or lovely?

The God of garden parties and seaside dances and tabernacles. The God who came as a baby and welcomed the so-called

outsiders and feasted with the forgotten. The God whose communities crowded around tables and pulled up more seats. The God who is always faithful and insists on belonging.

A forever wedding feast is just the sort of forever our God would insist on, isn't it? And just like real-life weddings, the wedding feast John daydreamed included an invitation. And the words on the invitation should sound quite familiar to you by now:

God's Spirit and God's friends say, "Come!"

Let anyone who hears this say, "Come!"

The gates to God's kingdom are always open, and the waters of life are free. Everyone is invited to come and fill up on the gift of God's goodness.

God is saying, "I Belong with you, and you Belong with me. Nothing can stop my love."

Can you imagine how John must have felt, shaking into awareness after that magnificent vision? He wrote down everything he saw, sealed it up, and mailed it to his friends all over the world who were struggling to trust God in the very messy middle. Which is exactly where we find ourselves today, in the kingdom of Already and Almost. And as we've seen, just because we know the end of the story doesn't make the messy middle go away.

You see, God has been inviting us into belonging from the very beginning, through many different stories and circumstances. They stretch into many, many yesterdays and will continue on into all the tomorrows.

And the stories we are writing today are the stories of the messy middle. Through the way he was born, the way he lived and loved, and even the way he died, Jesus showed us how to live here in the messy middle. With heaven and earth, hope and sorrow. He sent us the Holy Spirit

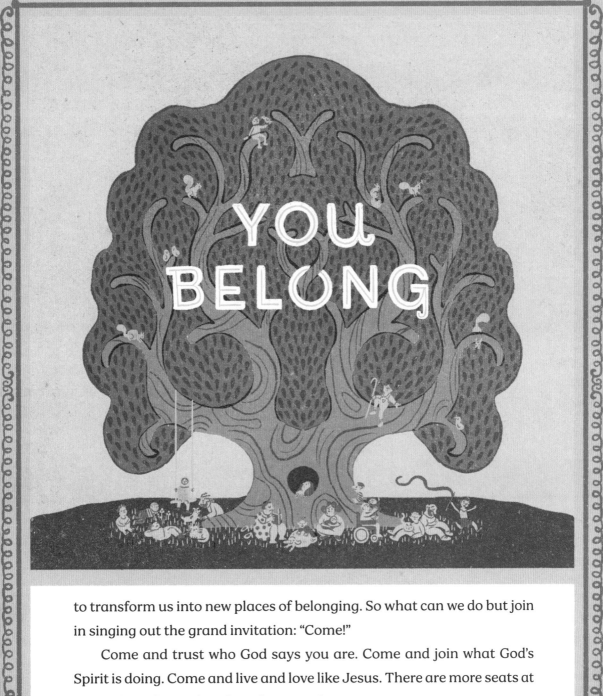

YOU
BELONG

to transform us into new places of belonging. So what can we do but join in singing out the grand invitation: "Come!"

    Come and trust who God says you are. Come and join what God's Spirit is doing. Come and live and love like Jesus. There are more seats at the table and you, dear friend—you Belong.

WONDER MOMENT

WHAT IS HEAVEN LIKE? AND WHAT WILL WE BE LIKE when we're there? Just like God, heaven—and our heavenly bodies—can't be fully described by our teensy human words or imaginings. All we have are peeks and promises.

The Bible tells us that Jesus's resurrected body still had scars. It also says that heaven will be a place of celebration and delight, an end to tears, suffering, and pain.

But what does all that mean? A person might say, "My skin will sparkle, and I'll eat pizza with Grandma!" Another might declare, "I'll walk again!" Someone else might announce, "I'll finally feel like I fully belong, just as I am."

What about you? What tears will God wipe from your eyes? What will make you sing glad songs or dance like you're at a wedding feast? What can you imagine that will fill you with delight, love, and belonging?

Our illustration of heaven explores glimpses from the Bible and imaginings from grown-ups and kids we love who have bodies of all shapes, sizes, and abilities. What do you notice in our picture? What would you add? What would you change?

As you spend time looking at our images (and maybe draw one of your own!), take some time to wonder about heaven and the grand invitation God extends to all of us.

ACKNOWLEDGMENTS

A special thank-you to our advisors:

Jennifer Garcia Bashaw

Courtney Buggs

Michelle Eastman

Elle Grover Fricks

Tatum Tricarico

NOTES

CHAPTER 2: For more information about the many Hebrew words for *sin,* I highly recommend Elle Grover Fricks's presentation in Brent Billings and Elle Grover Fricks, "294: John—Sacrifice, Suffering, and Joy," September 2, 2022, in *The BEMA Podcast.* For a higher-level view of sin as the opposite of God's dream, see John Goldingay, *Old Testament Theology: Israel's Faith,* Old Testament Theology Series, vol. 2 (Downers Grove, Ill.: InterVarsity, 2016).

CHAPTERS 7 AND 8: The contrasting themes of *empire* versus *shalom* are laid out beautifully in season 1 of *The BEMA Podcast,* which contains plenty of excellent text recommendations.

CHAPTER 19: For more information on Judean monarchs, including queen regents such as Jedidah, check out Dr. Wilda Gafney's research in *Womanist Midrash: A Reintroduction to the Women of the Torah and the Throne* (Louisville, Ky: Westminster John Knox, 2017).

CHAPTER 24: For more information about the fascinating research behind the word *Magdalene,* check out Elizabeth Schrader and Joan E. Taylor, "The Meaning of 'Magdalene': A Review of Literary Evidence," *Journal of Biblical Literature* 140, no. 4 (December 2021): 751–73.

CHAPTER 27: For a more complete picture of that "lion's paw moment," please enjoy the poem *Osso Buco,* by Billy Collins, Poetry Foundation, *Poetry Magazine,* August 1993.

CHAPTER 29: When exploring theology regarding disabilities, a good first step is to learn about the medical models of disability versus social ones. My interpretation of this and other stories about disability assumes the social model. If you would like to read more about this topic, please see these titles:

- Sarah J. Melcher, Mikeal C. Parsons, and Amos Yong, *The Bible and Disability: A Commentary,* Studies in Religion, Theology, and Disability (Waco, Tex.: Baylor University Press, 2017).

- Kathy Black, *A Healing Homiletic: Preaching and Disability* (Nashville: Abingdon, 1996).

- Amy Kenny, *My Body Is Not a Prayer Request: Disability Justice in the Church* (Grand Rapids, Mich.: Brazos, 2022).

CHAPTER 32: For some interesting research about the character we call *Martha,* check out Elizabeth Schrader's article "Was Martha of Bethany Added to the Fourth Gospel in the Second Century?," *Harvard Theological Review* 110, no. 3 (July 2017): 360–92.

MARIKO CLARK is a Japanese American author, mother, and storyteller on a mission to help kids embrace diversity and wonder. Her time as an editor with National Geographic Learning sharpened her ability to make complex topics accessible and engaging. She equips kids and caregivers with spiritual resources to navigate the messy middle, wrestle with tough questions, and find community in the journey. Mariko lives outside of Indianapolis with her husband and three sweet and spicy kids.

RACHEL ELEANOR is an illustrator known for doodles of questing travelers, friendly spirits, and all manner of creatures. She uses drawing as a way to explore the wilderness within and without, focusing on themes of spirituality and mindfulness. Her whimsical characters have inhabited books and stationery, championed brands, and even bedecked beverages. She lives in Atlanta with her husband, son, and tabby cat, where they enjoy taking long walks, picking flowers, and cooking with their friends.

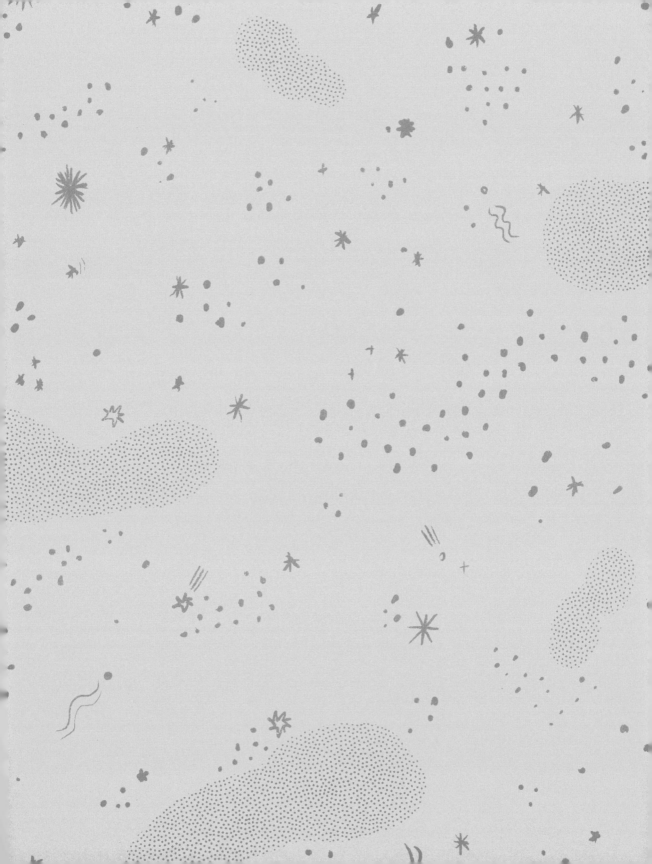

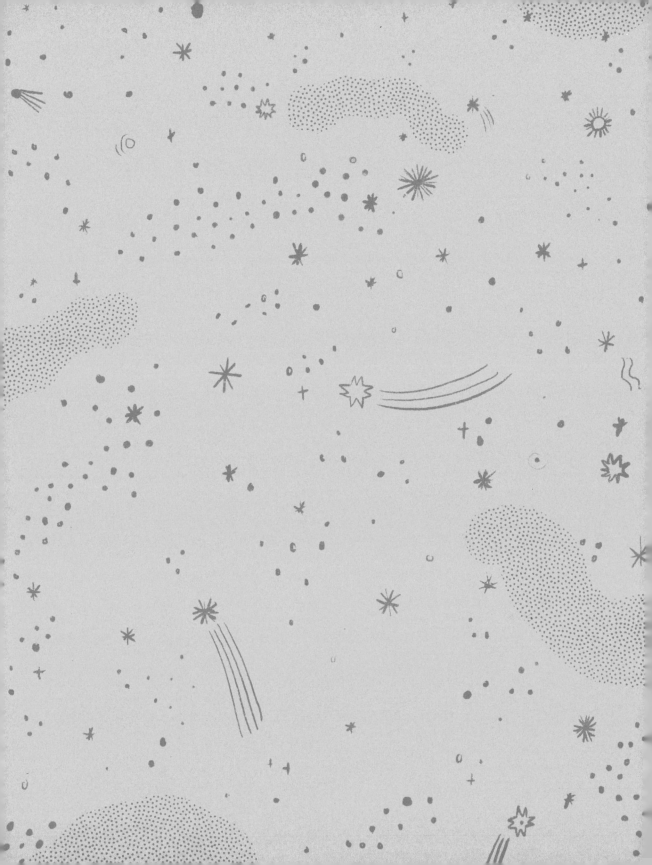